The Philosophy of Well-Being

Well-being occupies a central role in ethics and political philosophy, including in major theories such as utilitarianism. It also extends far beyond philosophy: recent studies on the science and psychology of well-being have propelled the topic to centre stage, and governments spend millions on promoting it. We are encouraged to adopt modes of thinking and behaviour that support individual well-being or 'wellness'.

What is well-being? Which theories of well-being are most plausible? In this rigorous and comprehensive introduction to the topic, Guy Fletcher unpacks and assesses these questions and many more, including:

- Are pleasure and pain the only things that affect well-being?
- Is desire-fulfilment the only thing that makes our lives go well?
- Can something be good for someone who does not desire it?
- Is well-being fundamentally connected to a distinctive human nature?
- Is happiness all that makes our lives go well?
- Is death necessarily bad for us?
- How is the well-being of a whole life related to well-being at particular times?

Also included is a glossary of key terms, and annotated further reading and study and comprehension questions follow each chapter, making *The Philosophy of Well-Being* essential reading for students in ethics and political philosophy, and also suitable for those in related disciplines such as psychology, politics and sociology.

Guy Fletcher is a Lecturer in Philosophy at the University of Edinburgh, UK. His current research is in metaethics, moral psychology and political philosophy. He is also the editor of *The Routledge Handbook of Philosophy of Well-Being* (2016).

The Philosophy of Well-Being

An introduction

Guy Fletcher

Routledge
Taylor & Francis Group

LONDON AND NEW YORK

First published 2016
by Routledge
2 Park Square, Milton Park, Abingdon, Oxon OX14 4RN

and by Routledge
711 Third Avenue, New York, NY 10017

Routledge is an imprint of the Taylor & Francis Group, an informa business

© 2016 Guy Fletcher

The right of Guy Fletcher to be identified as the author of this work has been asserted by him in accordance with sections 77 and 78 of the Copyright, Designs and Patents Act 1988.

British Library Cataloguing in Publication Data
A catalogue record for this book is available from the British Library

Library of Congress Cataloging in Publication Data
Names: Fletcher, Guy, 1983- author.
Title: The philosophy of well-being : an introduction / by Guy Fletcher.
Description: 1 [edition]. | New York : Routledge, 2016. | Includes bibliographical references and index.
Identifiers: LCCN 2015040250| ISBN 9781138818347 (hardback : alk. paper)
ISBN 9781138818354 (pbk. : alk. paper) | ISBN 9781315745329 (e-book)
Subjects: LCSH: Well-being.
Classification: LCC BD431 .F54 2016 | DDC 171/.3--dc23
LC record available at http://lccn.loc.gov/2015040250

ISBN: 978-1-138-81834-7 (hbk)
ISBN: 978-1-138-81835-4 (pbk)
ISBN: 978-1-315-74532-9 (ebk)

Typeset in Times New Roman
by Taylor & Francis Books

Contents

Acknowledgement

For written comments on various drafts of this work I am extremely grateful to: Daniel Groll, Benjamin Yelle, Eden Lin, Connie Rosati, Alex Gregory, Alex Sarch, Tim Taylor, Debbie Roberts, Rick Sendelbeck, Gwen Bradford, Richard Kim, Ben Bramble, Chris Woodard.

There are an enormous number of people whom I should thank for stimulating conversations or email exchanges on these issues. In addition to the above, these include: Jacob Edwards, Brad Hooker, Philip Stratton-Lake, John Cottingham, Jonathan Dancy, Jussi Suikkanen, Francesco Orsi, Valerio Salvi, Fiona Woollard, Alex Gregory, John Midgley, Richard Kraut, Steve Campbell, Alex Sarch, Brad Cokelet, Jennifer Hawkins, Chris Heathwood, Dale Dorsey, Daniel Halliday, Talbot Brewer, Anne Baril, Allan Hazlett, Jason Raibley, Hallie Liberto, Janice Dowell, Mike Ridge, Patrick Todd, Elinor Mason, Matthew Chrisman, Kenneth Walden, Alan Wilson, Alfred Archer, Silvan Wittwer and others I have surely forgotten (please accept my apologies!).

I must also thank my students from Exeter College, Oxford (2009–2011) and from University of Edinburgh (2011–), along with Alex Sarch's students from University of Southern California (who were guinea-pigs for a draft version of the book), for a cavalcade of helpful questions, suggestions and confusions.

Tony Bruce and Adam Johnson at Routledge were tremendously helpful, as were a raft of referees for the proposal and the final version, each of whom made innumerable improvements.

The final debt to acknowledge is to Debbie and Elijah Roberts, each of whom gives my life a continual uphill curve.

Introduction

From the fact that you are reading this introduction it is fairly safe to assume that your life is going reasonably well. You have access to books, you have the linguistic and other capacities with which to read them, and you have the free time to do so. Such has not been true of the majority of people who have ever lived.

You might wonder what I mean in saying that your life is going reasonably well and that other people's lives do (did) not. The relevant kind of evaluation I am making is in terms of *well-being*, about how well lives go *for the person who lives them*. But you might wonder what well-being *is*. One thing I could do to try to help here is to point you to a string of synonyms ('welfare', 'prudential value', 'self-interest', 'utility') and you might find that somewhat helpful. But you might *still* be a little unsure or sceptical about the idea of someone's life going well or going badly. Let me say a little more.

Some people's lives go extremely well. They are born into happy families, they secure good educations, make friends, pursue interesting and rewarding work, enjoy pleasurable hobbies, have loving and supportive families. Other lives go extremely badly. Here are two descriptions of such lives. The first, a description of nineteenth-century English peasant life:

> His sire was a pauper, and his mother's milk wanted nourishment. From infancy his food has been bad as well as insufficient; and he now feels the pains of unsatisfied hunger nearly whenever he is awake. But half-clothed, and never supplied with more warmth than suffices to cook his scanty meals, cold and wet come to him, and stay by him with the weather. He is married, but he has not tasted the highest joys of husband and father. His partner, and little ones being, like himself, often hungry, seldom warm, sometimes sick without aid, and always sorrowful without hope, are greedy, selfish, and vexing; so, to use his own expression, he 'hates the sight of them', and resorts to his hovel, only because a hedge affords less shelter from the wind and rain. He must support his family, though he cannot do so. This brings begging, trickery, and quarrelling; and ends in settled craft. Though he have the inclination, he wants the courage to become, like more energetic men of his class, a poacher or smuggler on a large scale; but he pilfers occasionally, and teaches his children to lie and steal. His subdued and slavish manner toward his great

neighbours shows that they treat him with suspicion and harshness. Consequently, he at once dreads and hates them; but he will never harm them by violent means. Too degraded to be desperate, he is thoroughly depraved. His miserable career will be short; rheumatism and asthma are conducting him to the workhouse, where he will breathe his last without one pleasant recollection, and so make room for another wretch who may live and die in the same way.[1]

Here is a second, a description of what life was like for women who suffered internment in the Gulag:

Many women's first memories of the Gulag tell of their fear, embarrassment and degradation. On arrival at their assigned camp, women were generally led to the bathhouse where they had a rare opportunity to wash. This was often an embarrassing and shocking experience. One former zek recalled how: 'The personnel were all male. You had to overcome the shame and humiliation, clench your teeth and control yourself, to endure the dirty jokes calmly and not spit at those hideous faces, or punch them between the eyes'... The humiliation did not stop there: guards often exploited the situation to 'inspect' the new arrivals, as women were a rarity within the Gulag...The disinfection of prisoners' clothing was generally ineffective anyway as the water used to wash the clothes was often not hot enough to kill the parasites and merely served to excite them further. In order to reduce the incidence of lice, women therefore endured further embarrassment as their heads and pubis were shaved. This procedure was supposed to be carried out by a female doctor, but they were rarely available, so male guards and doctors gleefully stepped in...Some women resisted: 'I was so shocked about it that at first I refused...soldiers kept my hands behind my back, while another forced my legs apart'. But women also had to submit to regular physical searches: 'They searched our hair, our mouths and even our...[they] were carried out solely to frighten and humiliate us'...Pregnancy could save a woman from beatings and even from execution. Rumours circulated that pregnancy could ensure an early release, as amnesties for pregnant women were implemented at various points. However, pregnancy was seen as a camp offence and many inmates were forced to have abortions, even though the practice was made illegal in the Soviet Union in 1936. Camp officials often took the decision to forcibly terminate a woman's pregnancy so that she could continue to work, in the interests of reaching production targets. There were also some women who attempted to end unwanted pregnancies themselves: Anna Andreevna talks of how she witnessed one woman stabbing herself with needles until she began bleeding heavily, signifying the end of her pregnancy. Even those terminations performed by camp doctors were often unskilled and dangerous. Therefore, pregnancy could be a scary time for expectant mothers. The survival rate of babies born in the Gulag was extremely low and children were often born in terrible, unhygienic conditions. Hava Volovich recalled her experience of giving birth to a daughter in the Gulag: 'She was born in a remote camp barracks, not in the medical block. There were three mothers there, and we were given a tiny room to ourselves...bedbugs poured from the ceiling and walls; we spent the whole night brushing them off the child. During the day we had to go to work and leave the infants with any old woman...these women would calmly help themselves to the food we left for the children.'[2]

I hope you agree that the lives described in these passages went *badly* (at least within the periods described, a qualification I hereafter leave implicit) and that features of the situations were extremely *bad for* the people within them. In saying that these lives went badly I do not mean that these people were *morally* bad. The first description contains some suggestions of moral vice, perhaps, but nothing in the second tells us about the moral goodness or badness of the people in the situation; they could have been perfect saints. What I mean is that these lives went badly *for the people who lived them*.

Here is another way to get well-being in focus. Suppose that you have a medical condition that has contaminated your blood and that can be cured in two different ways

   i   receiving a blood donation

OR

   ii   receiving a new kidney.

As your friend I am compelled to help. It turns out that I am a compatible donor for each of blood and kidney. Let us assume that you will be cured completely by either treatment (and that the risk of failure is identical in each case). Now let us look at the two options. Donating my kidney is *much* more painful and much more time-consuming. It also has a much longer recovery period. Donating blood, by contrast, is only slightly painful, takes hardly any time, and leaves me with two kidneys.

In light of these facts, it seems that we can conclude that each option is equally good *for you*.[3] By contrast, donating my kidney is much more *costly* to me than simply donating my blood. It is worse *for me* to donate my kidney than to lose some blood.

The kind of value that we are thinking about when we try to determine whether the blood donation is better for me than the kidney donation is that of prudential value, of well-being, of how well my life goes for me. Another way to put the point is that the *currency* in which the blood donation is better for me than the kidney donation is the currency of my well-being.

Here is one final way to get well-being in focus. You are 25 and you now face a choice between two different careers. You could be in a rock band or you could be a researcher into fundamental physics (your talents are diverse!).

To get around the issue of uncertainty, let us suppose that we have the full facts about what those two lives would be like (but your memory will be wiped after making the choice).

Suppose that the life in the rock band would be unbelievably *fun*. You would spend a lot of time playing music you love, you would spend time with your friends, you would see the world, attend all of the best parties, and visit far flung places. You would top the charts in every major country with your first album. However, despite once being extremely popular, your band would be a victim of changes in musical taste and so your career would be over at 40. Furthermore, the years of excess would take their toll and so you would experience five years of ill health before dying alone at 45.

By contrast, life as a research scientist would be extremely intellectually rewarding. You would spend a lot of time thinking about and researching issues that are fundamental to the nature of the universe and that you therefore find extremely interesting. You would make discoveries about the fundamental nature of the universe, writing academic books whose influence, though modest, lasts for centuries. Your life would be comparatively solitary. You would have professional acquaintances with whom you are friendly but beyond your life partner and children you have few firm friends. However, your life would afford space for leisure time and for healthy habits and you would be active right up until your peaceful death at 70.

These two lives are very different and we can evaluate them in lots of different ways. But focusing exclusively on their prudential value, on how good they would be for the person who lives them, which would you rather live? If you have difficulty answering this question, this reflects the difficulty of comparing these lives when it comes to well-being or prudential value. It is hard to decide *how* good each of these lives would be for the person who lives them and, thus, which would be better for them to live. The difficulty you are facing is the difficulty of determining how well each life goes, with respect to well-being.

Terminology

Let me say something about the terminology I will use in this book (students, entirely reasonably, often find the range of terminology employed in discussions of well-being a little bewildering). I will sometimes simply talk about something being good (or bad) for someone. For example, 'pleasure is good for me', 'pain is bad for me'. I will sometimes put points in terms of prudential value and disvalue. For example, 'pleasure has prudential value' and 'pain has prudential disvalue'. I might also talk about what *enhances* well-being and what *detracts* from it. For example, 'pleasure enhances well-being' and 'pain detracts from well-being'. Finally, I will sometimes talk about things benefitting or harming. For example, 'pleasure benefits those who experience it' and 'pain harms those who experience it'. I will treat these as mere stylistic variants.[4]

Outline of the book

Overall structure

The first four chapters cover the most commonly discussed and most historically influential theories of well-being: hedonism, desire-fulfilment theory, objective list theory and perfectionism.[5] Chapters 5 and 6 cover two theories which are in some ways more recent additions to the suite of theories, theories which are for that reason less mapped out and understood. The first is the happiness theory of well-being,[6] the other is the idea of a hybrid theory of well-being. Chapters 7 and 8 move away from particular theories of well-being to examine issues about well-being, lives and death.

Chapter summary

In the first chapter we examine hedonism about well-being. Roughly, the view claims that only pleasure is ultimately good for us and that only pain is ultimately bad for us. Such a theory has a lot going for it. Many cases of pleasure seem obviously to be good for us. And many cases of pain seem obviously to be bad for us. Nonetheless, hedonism faces a significant set of challenges, challenges that suggest that pleasure and pain alone are not the only things that are good and bad for us.

In chapter 2, we move on to discuss desire-fulfilment theories of well-being, theories that claim that what is good for us is what fulfils our desires (and that what is bad for us is what frustrates them). It seems intuitively very plausible that getting what we want is good for us and that failing to get what we want is bad for us. But such theories face challenges. In their most basic forms they seem to generate implausible results. This requires further development and refining of the theory.

Chapter 3 examines objective list theories of well-being, theories that claim that things are good or bad for people independently of their desiring them or being averse to them. As we shall see, such theories have certain virtues but face important challenges. These include the claim that such theories are arbitrary or problematically alienating. This objection is discussed in the chapter. Then, in an appendix to chapter 3, I revisit the alienation objection to objective-list theories and try to show a range of different ways in which one could interpret the idea that a theory of well-being can be alienating.

In chapter 4 we examine the credentials of 'perfectionist' theories of well-being. These theories postulate a significant connection between (i) what is good for humans and (ii) human nature (and so on for other kinds of animals).

In chapters 5 and 6 we examine two alternate theories of well-being. The first, the happiness theory of well-being, claims that happiness (alone) contributes to well-being. A major part of assessing this theory consists in the job of looking at different theories of the nature of happiness. For that reason we spend some time examining theories of the nature of happiness.

Chapter 6 is the final chapter dealing with theories of well-being. Therein we look at a very recent development: hybrid theories of well-being. Such theories try to combine two theories to generate more complex, but hopefully more plausible, theories of well-being. Whether such theories offer much promise of improving upon their constituent parts is a major question addressed by that chapter.

In chapter 7 we move away from looking at particular things that are good/bad for people (and why) or the prudential value of particular episodes and look instead at the prudential value of *lives* as a whole. In particular, we examine the claim that a person's lifetime well-being (how their life goes, in terms of well-being as a whole) is not determined in a simple additive fashion by how it goes at each point. This claim is called the 'shape of a life phenomenon'. In this chapter we examine the evidence for such a phenomenon.

Finally, in chapter 8 we move on to thinking about well-being and the end of life. In particular, whether death is bad for us, whether death harms us. As we see in that chapter, it is necessary to make clear exactly what the question is. There are a number of different ways to interpret the claim that death is a harm.

How this book is written

A large proportion of this book arose from undergraduate teaching. In that teaching I found it surprisingly difficult to (i) examine first hand the particular theories and claims offered by philosophers of well-being whilst also (ii) guiding the students to understand the relevant issues and how to *theorise* about well-being. Some of the difficulty is terminological. Some of it stems from differences in the theoretical or historical contexts of the discussions.

For that reason my lectures on well-being gradually evolved to a point where I introduce the theories and issues myself and then direct students to the relevant works of other philosophers. I largely preserve that style here. I think it is better that readers go away with a sense of what the relevant issues are and what the theories are like *in general* rather than focusing, from the outset, on the theories of particular philosophers. I explain the choice of style knowing that it might otherwise be misconstrued as the product of overconfidence. The truth is the exact opposite.

Finally: I have aimed to make this text as non-partisan as possible. But I have not aimed simply for straightforward comparative description. It would be underwhelming if the dialectic of the book was simply comparative: 'X argues p,q,r', 'Y argues a,b,c'. I also think that a *critical* discussion of the theories better equips students to *theorise* about well-being rather than to simply know what the different views are. For that reason whilst I do not try to settle what the truth about well-being is, I allow myself to argue and to claim that some theories have virtues and vices, that some objections are good, and that some others do not work. Of course you *must* ask yourself as you go along if you agree with me.

Notes

1 Attributed to 'A Liberal Member of Parliament (1830)' by Engels (1845).
2 http://gulaghistory.org/nps/onlineexhibit/stalin/women.php, accessed 11 June 2015.
3 Remember the stipulations above – the procedures have equal failure rates and either option will completely cure your condition (if successful).
4 To emphasise: there are other contexts where it might be useful or important to distinguish these.
5 Why this ordering? Students and instructors may wish only to cover the main theories – for example, on a course which is not focused exclusively on well-being – so I put these together in a group, for simplicity. Other ways of ordering the discussion would have the advantage of illuminating the similarities and differences between the theories. Many thanks to referees here for making me think about the ordering of the chapters.
6 I grant that it has long been common for people to use 'happiness' to talk about well-being.

References

Engels, F. (1845). 'The Condition of the Working Class in England'. https://www.marxists.org/archive/marx/works/1845/condition-working-class/ch12.htm, accessed 22 December 2015.

Online Exhibit. 'Gulag: Soviet Forced Labor Camps and the Struggle for Freedom'. http://gulaghistory.org/nps/onlineexhibit/stalin/women.php, accessed 11 June 2015.

1 Hedonism

1.1 Introduction

The simplest theory of well-being is hedonism.[1] This is the view that *pleasure* is the only thing with prudential value and *pain* the only thing with prudential disvalue. In more everyday terms, the hedonist thinks that all and only pleasure is good for you and that all and only pain is bad for you.

To avoid confusion, it is important to be clear that the hedonist makes these claims solely about what is *non-instrumentally* good for you and bad for you. The hedonist allows that things other than pleasure can be good for us *instrumentally*, things such as money, friendship, a nice house, and painkillers. But the hedonist will say that these things are good for us in a non-fundamental way because they are simply means to pleasure (or the avoidance of pain).

It is easy to see the appeal of hedonism. When we think about lives that are high in well-being, lives that seem to have gone well for the person who lives them, it is difficult to imagine them either lacking pleasure or being full of painful episodes. The paradigm cases of people whose lives are going well for them all experience great joy and pleasure in a wide range of things and experience little serious pain. Furthermore, when explaining why something would be good for someone the claim that they would *enjoy* it, that it would be pleasurable, seems obviously to be good evidence that it is good for them. Thus the pre-theoretical appeal of hedonism is clear.

It will be useful now to think a bit more precisely about hedonism and about the arguments for it. Here, first, is a more precise formulation of hedonism about well-being:

Hedonism:

1 All and only pleasure is (non-instrumentally) good for us.
2 All and only pain is (non-instrumentally) bad for us.
3 A person's overall level of well-being is determined solely by the balance of pleasure and pain they experience.[2]

(Henceforth I often omit the 'non-instrumentally', for the sake of readability. All claims about what is good for should be taken to be about what is *non-instrumentally* good for, unless otherwise specified.)

Questions left open

This formulation of hedonism is sufficiently precise for our purposes but it leaves open some questions. First, it says nothing about what pleasure or pain *are*. [3] Second, it does not tell us how to get precise answers about a person's well-being. It does not say exactly *how* the degree of prudential value of a pleasure is determined. It does not tell us, for example, how the *intensity* of a pleasure and its *duration* serve to determine its prudential value (and vice versa for pain). Although hedonists have assumed, reasonably, that increases in either duration or intensity make pleasures more prudentially valuable (and pains more prudentially disvaluable) hedonists have not much considered exactly how these factors interact. More than one view is possible here (one might give priority to intensity, or to duration, or endorse some complicated function of both).

Hedonic levels

It will be useful to talk about a person's hedonic level. By this I mean their *overall* balance of pleasure and pain. To get the idea, imagine that you are celebrating a recent success (a new job, finishing your degree, etc.), enjoying exquisite food and drink in the company of those you love. However, at the same time you have the painful soreness of a recently injured knee and your chair is rather uncomfortable. Thus whilst you experience pleasure from some aspects of your situation (the success, the food and drink, the company) you experience pain from others (your knee, the uncomfortable chair). The balance of the pleasure and pain that you experience is your *hedonic level* at that time.

If hedonism is true then it would follow that a person's hedonic level is perfectly *correlated with* their well-being. Any increase, or decrease, in the one would *necessarily* accompany an increase, or decrease, in the other. To put this less abstractly, if hedonism is true then all of the following are true:

1 If someone's hedonic level increases (they experience more pleasure and/ or less pain) then it must be the case that their level of well-being increases.
2 If someone's hedonic level decreases then it must be the case that their level of well-being decreases.
3 If someone's well-being increases then it must be the case that their hedonic level increases (they experience more pleasure and/or less pain).
4 If someone's well-being decreases then it must be the case that their hedonic level decreases.

Call the combination of claims (1)–(4) the *Perfect Hedonic Correlation* thesis.

1.2 Arguments for hedonism

Paradigm cases and correlation arguments

One kind of evidence that a hedonist can appeal to in support of the view is the correlation between a person's well-being and their hedonic level. For example:

> **Raj on the Rollercoaster**: Raj is enjoying a rollercoaster ride. Suddenly, a bird flies into his face, which is very painful. After getting off the ride Raj is given some painkillers which numb the area and he feels no pain. His friend then buys him candy floss, which he loves, and pleasurably eats.

The hedonist might ask us to observe that in this case it seems plausible both that

i   Raj's hedonic level starts off fairly high, decreases suddenly, and then increases again a little later.
ii Raj's well-being level starts off fairly high, decreases suddenly, and then increases again a little later.

They might then argue that the best *explanation* of this correlation between Raj's hedonic level and his level of well-being is that Raj's well-being is exclusively determined by his hedonic level. Put another way, this correlation occurs because only his hedonic level affects his well-being level.

This argument is overly ambitious. The case of Raj gives us evidence that pleasure and pain contribute to well-being. But it does not show that *only* pleasure and pain contribute to well-being. The correlation between hedonic level and well-being level observed does not show that *other* things could not have also contributed to (or detracted from) Raj's well-being.

To see this, imagine a variation of the case where we keep Raj's hedonic level the same but add to Raj's life that he has extra friendships, or that he is successful in his major life goals, that he is more self-confident, or that he has more knowledge. It seems at least plausible that for some such cases Raj has a higher level of well-being than in the original, even though his hedonic level is the same in both cases.

There is a second weakness in the argument from correlation. It will be easier to see the problem with that argument by finding the same fault in a related argument for hedonism, the argument from paradigm cases. This is the hedonist's claim that their view is supported by paradigm cases of people whose lives are going well. To put the argument formally, suppose the hedonist argues:

1   Paradigm cases of lives high in well-being all have high hedonic levels.
2   If the paradigm cases of lives high in well-being all have high hedonic levels then hedonism is true.

Therefore,

3   Hedonism is true.

This argument is valid. If the premises are true then the conclusion must be true. So if there is a problem with the argument it must be that one or more of the premises is false.

Though one might have doubts about premise (1) let us grant it for the sake of argument. The trouble comes from premise (2). The fact that paradigmatic cases of lives with high levels of well-being also have high hedonic levels is not *sufficient* to show that hedonism is true. Paradigm cases of lives high in well-being may have *other*, non-hedonic, features that explain their high levels of well-being. So whilst there might be a correlation between hedonic levels and high levels of well-being, a person's hedonic level may not *determine* their level of well-being. This is because we cannot *always* conclude from a correlation between two variables that one of them explains the other.

Here is an example of how correlation between two variables does not allow us to safely conclude that one explains the other. My thermometer says '23 degrees' and it is 23 degrees. Later it says '21 degrees' and it is 21 degrees. There is thus a correlation between (i) the reading on my thermometer and (ii) the temperature. But we cannot conclude from this that the thermometer reading determines the temperature. That would be a mistake.

Sometimes we observe a correlation between two variables where we should conclude that *neither* explains the other. For example, consider the apparent correlation between (a) the rate of drownings in outdoor swimming pools and (b) ice-cream sales.[4] Increases and decreases in (a) correlate with increases and decreases in (b). Should we therefore conclude that drownings determine ice-cream sales (or vice versa)? Definitely not. So why are these two things correlated? Because a third variable – temperature – determines *both* the rate of drownings and ice cream sales. As temperatures go up more people eat ice cream and more people use, and get into difficulties in, outdoor swimming pools. So whilst there is a correlation between (a) and (b) neither explains the other. They are instead both explained by some third factor.

How can we use this idea of spurious (non-explanatory) correlations against the argument above? The answer is that we can use this observation to undermine premise (2) from the argument by pointing out that even if there is a correlation between hedonic level and well-being level (i.e. premise (1) is true) this *may* be explained by some third factor. (We will see an example of a candidate third factor in the next chapter, on desire-fulfilment theory.)

For now we can conclude two things. First, the case of Raj does not rule out things other than pleasure or pain from affecting well-being. Second, whilst the correlation between paradigmatic cases of lives high in well-being and lives with a high hedonic level provide *some* evidence for hedonism it does not by itself entitle us to conclude that hedonism is true. This is because the correlation in question might be explained by some third variable.

Welfare subjects and pleasure and pain

Another kind of evidence that hedonists could appeal to in support of hedonism is the clear overlap between (i) things that can have a level of well-being ('welfare subjects') and (ii) things that experience pleasure and pain. Whilst it is implausible that pencils, telephones and lampshades have levels of well-being, it is extremely plausible that gorillas, dolphins and dogs are welfare subjects, that they have levels of well-being. Given that the former set of things cannot experience pleasure and pain but that the latter can, this is some evidence for hedonism.

One reply that non-hedonists will make is that the sets of things that do and do not plausibly have levels of well-being have *other* features that explain the division between them. For example, pencils, telephones and lampshades are also incapable of desire, friendship, knowledge and achievement, whereas gorillas, dolphins and dogs plausibly are capable of at least a number of these things, if not all. Thus, it is not clear that this division (between things that are plausibly capable of well-being and things that are not) tracks *only* whether the relevant things can experience pleasure and pain. Nonetheless, because it is relatively uncontroversial that the kinds of things that can have a level of well-being are also the kinds of things that can experience pleasure and pain, hedonism has a very clear, plausible, answer to the question of why some things are welfare subjects and some are not. This is some evidence in favour of hedonism.

Motivational arguments

A third kind of argument that might be given for hedonism relies upon two claims about motivation. The first is that all action maximises self-interest (or at least aims to maximise self-interest). The second is that pleasure and pain are the *only* things capable of motivating us to act.

1 All human action aims to maximise well-being.
2 The agent's pleasure and pain are the only things capable of motivating them.

Therefore,

3 Hedonism is true.

Various responses are possible here. One is that (1) and (2) do not straightforwardly entail (3) so there is work to do to show that the argument is valid (that the conclusion must be true if the premises are true).[5] But more importantly each of the first two premises of the argument is *highly* controversial.

It is *prima facie* implausible that agents always aim to maximise their own self-interest. Taking some everyday cases, we often seem to act against our own interests. We give money to charity (when no one is looking). We return property to people who have dropped it. To take more extreme examples, people often make great sacrifices to save others, knowing that it will certainly result in grave harm or death for themselves. Take soldiers who throw themselves on grenades to prevent harm to their fellow soldiers. To think that all such cases are *really* cases where people are trying (but spectacularly failing) to maximise their self-interest seems highly implausible.

It is also *prima facie* implausible that agents are motivated only by the prospect of their own pleasure or avoidance of pain. Is it really true that *nothing* else in the world motivates us to act? Take a case where you are walking along and see someone fall over. Aren't you sometimes motivated just by the thought that someone needs help? Don't people sometimes act from a sense of duty, or because they want to help a friend, or because they want to preserve something important for future generations?[6]

Fully assessing these two premises here would take us too far afield. I simply note that this is one possible argument for hedonism. It is, I think, one that is implicit in some people's thought when thinking about hedonism. But it is an argument that requires *a lot* of support, given its contentious premises.

Experience requirement

A fourth reason that hedonists might give in support of their view is that hedonism nicely captures the idea that there is an *experience requirement* on well-being. This is the idea that what is good and bad for you must be experience affecting. To put this claim more precisely, a hedonist might argue that the following is true:

> **Experience requirement**: if something contributes to someone's well-being it must affect their experience in some way.

They might then point out that pleasure and pain meet this experience requirement. This is because pleasure and pain necessarily affect experience. They might then conclude that the truth of the experience requirement, coupled with pleasure and pain satisfying the requirement, shows that hedonism is true.

One way to resist this argument is to question the experience requirement itself. That is, we might question whether everything that impacts upon a person's well-being must impact upon their experience. Here is one reason to doubt it. Take two possible lives with the same hedonic level at each moment (call the people leading these lives Raj 1 and Raj 2). Suppose, though, that whilst Raj 1's life is actually as it appears to him to be, Raj 2's life is actually an elaborate sham perpetrated by his so-called friends and family. Though they secretly despise him they find it much funnier to pretend that they really love him and enjoy spending time with him in order to then mock his naiveté when he is absent.

Raj 2's life seems to be going worse for him than Raj 1's life is for him. If that is true then at least some aspects of well-being are things that do not affect the person's experience. After all, Raj 1 and 2 have the same hedonic levels, and Raj 2 never learns about the false life he leads – so their lives are experientially identical. Nevertheless, Raj 2's life is plausibly going worse for him than Raj 1's life is going for him. In light of this kind of case we might question the experience requirement in general.

We might also question how strongly the experience requirement supports *hedonism* in particular (i.e. how strongly it supports hedonism over other theories of well-being). After all, pleasure and pain aren't the *only* things that affect our experience. To give two examples, happiness and self-respect seem to be (a) distinct from pleasure and (b) things that affect our experience.[7] And it is at least prima facie plausible that happiness and self-respect contribute to well-being. So even if the hedonist is correct to hold:

i   that pleasure and pain affect our experience

AND

ii   that anything that affects well-being must affect an individual's experience

it *still* does not follow that hedonism is true. There may be other, non-hedonic, goods compatible with the experience requirement.

Having explained some of the arguments for hedonism I now turn to objections to the view.

1.3 Objections to hedonism

The experience machine

In *Anarchy, State and Utopia*, Robert Nozick presents the following case in discussing hedonism:

> Suppose there were an experience machine that would give you any experience you desired. Superduper neuropsychologists could stimulate your brain so that you would think and feel you were writing a great novel, or making a friend, or reading an interesting book. All the time you would be floating in a tank, with electrodes attached to your brain. Should you plug into this machine for life, preprogramming your life experiences?...You can pick and choose from their large library or smörgåsbord of such experiences, selecting your life's experiences for, say, the next two years. After two years have passed, you will have ten minutes or ten hours out of the tank, to select the experiences of your next two years. Of course, while in the tank

you won't know that you're there; you'll think that it's all actually happening.[8]

Nozick's example is extremely engaging but features of the example introduce complications, some of which are potentially distracting. For that reason let me give a 'tidied up' version of the experience machine case before explaining what exactly it purports to show. (The case I give is similar to the variant cases of Raj above.)

> **Trudy and Flora**: Trudy lives in New York. When not carrying on her ground-breaking research into stem cell treatment, she enjoys running marathons, working for a local charity, skiing, socialising with friends and spending time with her life partner and their children. She also somehow finds time to pen highly successful, critically acclaimed, novels. She enjoys great physical health and springs out of bed every morning full of joy and excitement.
>
> Now meet Flora. When Flora was born she was attached to a machine that produces sensory stimulation and that gives her very rich, vivid, and life-like experiences. She has the pleasurable experience of carrying on ground-breaking research into stem cell treatment, of running marathons, of working for a local charity, skiing, socialising with friends and spending time with her life partner and their children. She also has the experience of writing highly successful and critically acclaimed novels. She is kept physically healthy by the machine and she also has the experience of springing out of bed every morning full of joy and excitement.

Let us stipulate that Trudy and Flora have lives of identical length and that their hedonic levels are identical at every moment of these lives. What does hedonism say about these two lives? Clearly, hedonism must conclude from the fact that Trudy and Flora have identical hedonic levels and that they have identical levels of well-being. Furthermore, given the facts of their lives they both live lives that are equally *high* in well-being.

What should we conclude about hedonism from the case of Flora? Some will think that pleasurable experiences that are generated this way have little prudential value (perhaps, even, that they have prudential *disvalue*). Some will think that Flora lives an utterly wretched awful life. These claims might be true. But they are much more controversial than the following claim, a claim that itself provides a strong reason to doubt hedonism. It is implausible that Trudy and Flora have *equal* levels of well-being. *Whatever* level of well-being one thinks is plausible for Trudy, it seems highly counterintuitive that Flora has that level of well-being also.

Some might think that Trudy and Flora *do* have equal levels of well-being. But suppose that one must choose which kind of life one's child would live (suppose that one's memory of making the choice would be immediately erased afterwards and one would have no possible contact with the child after making the choice). Shouldn't one choose for one's child the life of Trudy over the life of Flora? Plausibly so and this is because Trudy's life has a higher level of well-being.

Alternatively, consider a variant of the case where Flora's enjoys a *slightly* higher hedonic level over a short period. If hedonism is true then Flora has a higher level of well-being. But this seems implausible. Trudy's position seems much more desirable than Flora's. Her well-being seems higher.

Let us take stock. It is important not to overstate what experience machine type cases might show. The case of Trudy and Flora does not show that pleasure does not contribute to well-being. Further, we need not think that the pleasure enjoyed by Flora has zero prudential value. But the case does provide a strong objection to the claim that well-being is determined *entirely* by a person's hedonic level. Plausibly, Trudy's level of well-being is higher than Flora's (despite equality in hedonic level) because she enjoys *real* friendships, *real* achievement, knowledge, etc. As Nozick puts the point:

> [W]e want to *do* certain things, and not just have the experience of doing them...[W]e want to *be* a certain way, to be a certain sort of person.[9]

In brief, the lesson of the experience machine is that hedonism provides at best an incomplete account of well-being. Pleasure does seem to contribute to well-being but other things contribute to well-being aside from pleasure.

Hedonist replies to the experience machine

How might a hedonist reply to the experience machine argument? There is no point in the hedonist objecting to the weirdness or outlandishness of the example. The example is clearly coherent and that is enough for it to be capable of being an objection to hedonism. After all, hedonism is not supposed to just be true of the normal cases. It is supposed to be the truth about well-being in all cases. Similarly, there is no point in hedonists claiming that in fact the hedonic levels of Trudy and Flora would not be equal (on the grounds, for example, that 'Flora would somehow know that her experiences were bogus'). The equality of hedonic level is *stipulated* as part of the example and the stipulation seems perfectly coherent. And we can imagine less unusual cases of people with equal hedonic levels but who differ with respect to achievement, friendship, etc. And that is enough to put pressure on hedonism.

A better approach for the hedonist to use is to try to undermine our judgement that Trudy and Flora have unequal levels of well-being. There are a number of tactics they might employ.[10] First, hedonists might point out that humans are prone to the 'status quo bias', namely the mistake of giving undue weight to the option they believe to be the current state of affairs. Applied to this case the hedonist might argue that when thinking about the value of lives that are plugged into them we are guilty of giving undue weight to the fact that we are not currently plugged into experience machines.

A second way that hedonists can try to undermine the judgement that Trudy and Flora's lives have unequal levels of well-being is to point out that we do *not* seem to care, when thinking about the prudential of disvalue of *pain*, whether it is based on a real experience or a charade. A painful experience plugged into the experience machine seems *just as bad* as a painful experience in reality, other things equal. The hedonist might then argue that unless there is good reason to accept an asymmetry between pleasure and pain with respect to bogus experience then we should not think Trudy and Flora's lives have unequal levels of well-being.

One problem with this suggestion is that it does not tackle the thought that likely stands behind the judgement that Trudy and Flora's lives have unequal levels of well-being, namely that things *other than* pleasure and pain contribute to well-being. Someone might grant that all pleasure and pain is equally valuable whether or not it is based on real experiences yet *still* judge Trudy's level of well-being to be higher because of the non-hedonic differences between Trudy's life and Flora's.

A third way that the hedonist might try to dislodge the inequality judgement is by, first, pointing to the fact that people who are deceived tend to find out about this and experience pain and anguish and, then, arguing that when we think about Trudy and Flora's lives we are illegitimately assuming that Flora *knows* or, more likely, will find out about her deception and be very pained by it. This response is rather weak, and close to the first one suggested above. It relies upon the idea that when we think about the case of Trudy and Flora we are *simply unable* to stick to the stipulation that their hedonic levels are identical. But in the absence of evidence of such an inability the response is not powerful.[11]

Finally, some hedonists have taken to wielding evolutionary debunking arguments against the experience machine. To understand these arguments we need to know what a debunking argument is in general. A debunking argument aims to show that the *source* of some belief makes that belief illegitimate in some way (that it is false, that it is unjustified, or merely that it has less support or justification than previously suspected). Everyday examples of debunking arguments appear when people claim that some person holds some belief only because of their upbringing, or because it suits their interests, or because they have been indoctrinated. A general form of debunking argument is

1   Your belief that J stems from process P.
2   Beliefs that stem from process P are illegitimate.

Therefore

3   Your belief that J is illegitimate.

An *evolutionary* debunking argument in particular is one that claims that evolution is the problematic process P. The evolutionary debunking arguments given by hedonists against the experience machine objection suppose that our anti-hedonistic responses to the experience machine case are a by-product of evolution. Put briefly, the suggestion is that in our evolutionary history it was advantageous to *believe* that, e.g. friendship and achievement are good for us. Why so? Because having such beliefs tends to make us pursue friendship and achievement and this, in turn, improves our chances of survival and propagation. Thus creatures with these beliefs, or disposed to form them, were more likely to pass on their genetic material.

The crucial point that the hedonist will then press is that this story of *why* it was evolutionarily advantageous for us to believe these things (e.g. that friendship and achievement has prudential value) did not require that the beliefs be true. Even if hedonism is true it could still be very useful for creatures to (falsely) believe that friendship and achievement are prudentially valuable. Why? Because such creatures would more likely survive and pass on their genes for the reasons given above. There is no reason to think that the evolutionary processes that generated these evolutionarily advantageous beliefs were truth-tracking. So we should be suspicious of these beliefs.

Put very schematically, the argument would be this:

1   Your believing that things other than pleasure and pain affect well-being stems from non-truth-tracking, evolutionary, processes.
2   Beliefs that stem from non-truth-tracking processes are illegitimate.

Therefore,

3   Your belief that things other than pleasure and pain affect well-being is illegitimate.

There are many details one could explore here. The most important point is that this argument is a problematic weapon for the *hedonist* to deploy. To the extent that it is a good objection to the non-hedonist it is an even better objection to hedonism.[12] Why so?

Think of the overlap between pleasurable behaviours and evolutionarily advantageous behaviours. It is easy to think of behaviours that are both pleasurable and that it was evolutionarily advantageous for humans to engage in (having sex, eating, recreation) and, conversely, behaviours that are both painful and that it was evolutionarily disadvantageous for humans to engage in (damaging one's own body, starving oneself, attacking large predators). Given this fact, it seems that a plausible evolutionary debunking story can be told of why it was advantageous for humans to believe that *pleasure is good for them* and that this story (also) does not require that the belief was true. After all, creatures that had the belief (*pleasure is good for me*) were more likely to have sex, eat, engage in recreation and they thereby increased their chances of reproductive success.

The upshot of this is that *if* we should doubt, on evolutionary grounds, our non-hedonic judgements about well-being, we should also doubt our judgements that pleasure and pain are good and bad for us. To put it bluntly, *if* speculation about the evolutionary causes of our beliefs gives us reason to doubt that friendship and achievement are good for us, then we have just as much reason to be suspicious that pleasure is good for us, absent some relevant difference between the cases.

Base pleasures

Whilst the experience machine objection targeted the hedonists' claim that *only* pleasures contribute positively to well-being, the 'base pleasures objection', targets the claim that *all* pleasures contribute to well-being.

Some examples of the kinds of pleasures that feature in the base pleasures objection are:[13]

- immoral pleasures (e.g. pleasures connected to immoral actions – enjoyment of torture, or of watching torture)
- pleasures from trivial or low-brow sources (e.g. pleasures from watching reality TV)
- pleasures that are undignified (e.g. pleasure from wallowing in mud like a pig).[14]

As this list makes clear, quite a diverse array of pleasures might be mentioned by someone wielding the base pleasures objection. The basic form of the objection is as follows:

Base pleasures objection

1 If hedonism is true then all pleasures contribute to well-being.
2 If all pleasures contribute to well-being then *base* pleasures contribute to well-being.
3 Base pleasures do not contribute to well-being.

Therefore,

4 Hedonism is false.

(There is also a second version of the base pleasures objection, which I will discuss below.)

Replies to the base pleasures objection

With one exception, the standard hedonistic replies to the base pleasures objection involve accepting premise (2) but denying premise (3). What the hedonist does is to argue that premise (3) is false, and so the argument is unsound. The different ways of rejecting (3) revolve around the claim that when we think about cases of base pleasures, and form the judgement that they do not contribute to well-being, we are making some sort of mistake. What mistake might we be making?

I Instrumental disvalue distractions

One of the objections hedonists can make to the base pleasures objection is that our belief that base pleasures are not prudentially valuable is a mistaken judgement based on the expectation that such pleasures would lead to future harms.[15] For example, perhaps when we consider the case of the torturer we are illegitimately thinking about the consequences of having a sadistic character, of having few or no significant friendships or personal relationships, or the likely punishment or retribution such a person might face. We thus undervalue how prudentially good the pleasure is.

This objection has some merit. A sadistic character generally does have bad consequences for a person. But that fact is unlikely to dislodge the judgement that, e.g. pleasure from torture just is, itself, of no prudential value to the person who experiences it. Those who form that judgement are likely to hold that it is still true even if we are very careful to stipulate away all of these possible distractions.

2 Wrong kind of value judgement

A second, perhaps more persuasive, suggestion that the hedonist can make as to why we mistakenly believe premise (3) is that we are conflating two kinds of value. In thinking about these cases we are being distracted by the *moral* disvalue of such pleasures and mistaking this for a lack of *prudential* value. Put another way, the hedonist might claim that we are being distracted by the moral badness of such pleasures and mistakenly thinking that the pleasures lack prudential value. The hedonist might then maintain that if we keep in mind that we are considering *only* the prudential value of such pleasures then we will see that they really are prudentially valuable.

To make this a little more abstract, the hedonist might urge us to think more precisely about the case. They might claim that it is tempting to contrast the case of the person who takes pleasure in torture with the person who enjoys some perfectly innocent pursuit (playing music). But, so the hedonist might claim, if we make that comparison then the difference in the *moral* value of these pleasures might lead us to illegitimately ascribe a difference in their *prudential* value. They might then claim that what we should do instead is to compare the case of someone deriving pleasure from inflicting torture with the case of the person who tortures but without enjoying it, or who tortures and is pained by doing so:

CASE OF THE THREE TORTURERS

	Hedonic level
Torturer 1	+10
Torturer 2	0
Torturer 3	−10

When we think of the case of the three torturers, is it more plausible that the pleasure is good for the agent? One way to think about the question is to ask which torturer is *worst off prudentially* (other things are equal). Is it torturer 1, engaging in torture but enjoying it? Or would one be better off in torturer 2's situation, or even torturer 3's?

Focusing on the comparative question might help us to make some progress. I think at least some people who were inclined to doubt the prudential value of malicious pleasures in the original case will think that torturer 1 is best off and that this is fairly good evidence that torturer 1's pleasure is in fact prudentially valuable. Thus the focus on the comparative question will shift some people from holding premise (3). The trouble though is that for many people the comparative question will actually *enhance* their commitment to the correctness of premise (3). That is, those whose commitment to (3) was clear-minded – not based on some mistake such as a mistake in the kind of evaluation made – will likely hold that to take pleasure in something so depraved as torture is *bad for you*. One can imagine them replying that one should want to be torturer 2, perhaps even torturer 3, if faced with the grim choice of being in one of these three positions.

3 Qualitative hedonism

I mentioned above that there are two different arguments from base pleasures against hedonism. The argument from base pleasures given above worked by highlighting some problematic pleasures and arguing that such pleasures hold no prudential value and so hedonism is false. A different kind of base pleasures objection focuses more directly on the fact that hedonism ascribes equal prudential value to different pleasures. This variant argument runs as follows:

Base pleasures equality objection

1   If hedonism is true then all *equal-sized* pleasures contribute equally to well-being.
2   If all equal-sized pleasures contribute equally to well-being then base pleasures of a given size contribute to well-being as much as non-base pleasures of the same size.

3   Base pleasures of a given size do not contribute to well-being equally with non-base pleasures of the same size.

Therefore,

4   Hedonism is false.

The difference between this argument and the previous one might be difficult to see. To get a clearer idea, take the following pair of cases:

	Hedonic level
S wallows in mud like a pig for 3 hours	+10
S reads *Hamlet*	+10

Someone might object to hedonism not because it ascribes prudential value to each pleasure but, instead, because it says S would be *equally* well off wallowing in mud like a pig as reading *Hamlet*. Put another way, hedonism claims that the pleasures from wallowing in mud like a pig are just as valuable as the pleasures from reading *Hamlet*. The objector then claims that this result is implausible and that S would be better off reading *Hamlet*.

To see the difference between this objection and the previous one, notice that the objector need not claim that the pleasure derived from wallowing in mud like a pig has no value. They need only claim that this pleasure is not *equally* good for the agent as the pleasure from the more lofty pursuit.

The difference between these two base pleasure objections is not always clearly drawn but it is worth being clear given the *different* kinds of responses that hedonists might wish to make to the different objections.

What can a hedonist say in response to the *base pleasures equality objection*? Of course they can make some of the same responses featured. They can claim that the wielder of this objection is confusing the question of what is good for the agent with (e.g.) what it would be best to do overall. And perhaps someone who reads literature is more likely to generate well-being for others than someone who derives pleasure from wallowing in mud like a pig. Alternatively, the hedonist can claim that the likely consequences of reading literature are more positive *for the agent* than the likely results of wallowing in mud like a pig. That is to say, there might be more *instrumental* value to the pleasure of reading literature than the pleasure of wallowing like a pig. Why might this be so? Perhaps pleasures derived from literature are more easily recreated, or better enable us to derive further pleasures than the purely sensory ones. The hedonist might then claim that when we judge the sensory pleasure to be non-instrumentally inferior we are mistaking the greater *instrumental* value that is typical of pleasure derived from reading literature for a difference in non-instrumental value.

A more philosophically interesting move available to the hedonist is to, first, concede that the pleasure from wallowing in mud like a pig is less prudentially valuable (non-instrumentally) than the pleasure from reading *Hamlet* and, second, claim that this is no problem for hedonism because hedonism is consistent with rejecting the claim that equal-*sized* pleasures always have equal value. Looking back at the Base Pleasures Equality Objection, such a hedonist is rejecting premise (1) of that argument:

(1) If hedonism is true then all equal-sized pleasures contribute equally to well-being.

The idea of a form of hedonism which rejects (1) is famously associated with John Stuart Mill. As Mill puts the idea:

> It would be absurd to think that while, in estimating all other things, quality is considered as well as quantity, the estimation of pleasures should be supposed to depend on quantity alone.[16]

Mill held that pleasures had different levels of quality and that the value of a pleasure was determined not only by its quantity but also by its *quality*.

To return to the case above, a qualitative hedonist might claim that they can accommodate the judgement that the pleasure from reading *Hamlet* has more prudential value than the pleasure from wallowing in mud like a pig. The reason they will give is that the pleasure from reading *Hamlet* is of higher *quality*.

Mill's qualitative hedonism received a barrage of criticism.[17] A common objection is that it is inconsistent for a hedonist to think that pleasures can have different levels of quality. Why so? The thought behind the objection is as follows: if such *pleasures* have different values then this can *only* be because of the different levels of value in the respective *activities* that generate the pleasures. But if only pleasure has value then there are no differences in value in the activities that produce pleasure (because activities that produce pleasure are not, themselves, prudentially valuable).

One problem with this objection is that it presumes that qualitative hedonism can only treat differences in the quality of pleasure as differences in the activities that produce pleasure. But that seems to be only one way to interpret the idea of pleasures being of different quality. Why not think that it is the pleasures themselves that have different qualities?

Part of what is at issue here is something that we left aside at the beginning of the chapter: the *nature* of pleasure. One view is that pleasures are intrinsically homogeneous mental states, differing only with respect to intensity and duration. If one assumes that view of pleasure, then it makes sense to think that differences in quality of pleasure can only be differences in the value of the activities that produce them. With these background assumptions in place, qualitative hedonism can seem unmotivated and implausible. *Why* does it affect the prudential value of pleasure that it stem from one activity rather than another if the pleasures themselves are intrinsically homogeneous?

An alternative view – one that is perhaps the most intuitive way of understanding qualitative hedonism – is that pleasures are themselves *heterogeneous*.

That is, pleasures have different intrinsic natures. If so, the pleasure derived from reading *Hamlet* might be intrinsically different from that derived from wallowing in mud like a pig. If this is the correct view of pleasure then it seems like an open possibility that the different intrinsic natures of pleasure are, or produce, differences in the quality of those pleasures. Thus one could be a qualitative hedonist, and try to avoid the base pleasures equality objection, by claiming that pleasures have differing intrinsic natures.

1.4 Conclusion

In this chapter we have considered hedonism about prudential value. The hedonist view is that all and only pleasure is good for you and that all and only pain is bad for you. We then looked at some arguments for the view and some objections. The objections targeted different features of hedonism. One of them – the experience machine – targeted hedonism's claim that, necessarily, everyone at the same hedonic level has the same level of well-being. Others targeted the way that hedonism gives value, or equal value, to problematic kinds of pleasures.

It is worth noticing that none of these objections claimed that *no* pleasures and pain have prudential value and disvalue. That is, none of the objections above even purported to show that pleasures (pain) are never good (bad) for us. They only targeted the stronger claims definitive of hedonism, namely that all and only pleasure (pain) are good (bad) for us. In light of this we might conclude that pleasure and pain are at least sometimes prudentially valuable even if hedonism is not correct that they are the only things that affect well-being.

Comprehension questions

1 If hedonism is true, is money good for us in exactly the same way that pleasure is?
2 What would make it true that it is in a person's best interests not to smoke, if hedonism is true?
3 What, if anything, is problematic about Nozick's original experience machine example?
4 What is qualitative hedonism about prudential value? How does it differ from purely quantitative hedonism?

Notes

1 In this chapter I use 'hedonism' to refer only to hedonism about well-being, rather than any other kind of hedonism.
2 Throughout the chapter I will assume a certain view about timing, namely that a pleasure (pain) is good (bad) for you at the time at which it occurs.

3 On this see: Bramble (2013; 2016), Feldman (2004), Gosling (1969), Gregory (2016), Heathwood (2013), etc.
4 Example taken from: http://blogs.seattletimes.com/educationlab/2013/12/04/ice-cream-doesnt-cause-drowning-and-other-warnings-about-interpreting-data, accessed 22 December 2015.
5 What extra premise does the argument rest upon?
6 Another question prompted by the premise: If such a strong claim is true *why* is it true? Why can't we be motivated by anything else? Notice that someone providing this argument would need some independent support for premise (2), and so couldn't appeal to the truth of hedonism to justify it.
7 See e.g. Haybron (2008: chapter 4).
8 Nozick (1974: 42–45).
9 Ibid.: 43.
10 I briefly mention them here but leave their full development and assessment as an exercise to the reader.
11 One might also think that the reason we would be upset to discover that our lives are like this is because their being so would be bad for us. But the hedonist must deny this. For more discussion see Nagel (1970).
12 For more on this see Fletcher (2007).
13 Some instances of the objection do not distinguish these categories.
14 Example from Feldman (2004).
15 This is similar to the reply considered above, that reactions to the experience machine illegitimately smuggle in *instrumental* disvalues.
16 Mill (1863).
17 See, for example, Moore (2000 [1903]). For extensive discussion of these issues, see e.g. Feldman (2004).

References

Fletcher, Guy (2007). 'Wrongness, Welfarism and Evolution: Crisp on Reasons and the Good'. *Ratio*, 20(3): 341–347.
Haybron, Daniel M. (2008). *The Pursuit of Unhappiness: The Elusive Psychology of Well-Being* (Oxford University Press).

Hedonism

Crisp, Roger (2006a). 'Hedonism Reconsidered'. *Philosophy and Phenomenological Research*, 73(3): 619–645.
Crisp, Roger (2006b). *Reasons and the Good* (Oxford University Press).
Feldman, Fred (2004). *Pleasure and the Good Life: Concerning the Nature, Varieties and Plausibility of Hedonism* (Clarendon Press).
Gregory, Alex (2016). 'Hedonism' in G. Fletcher (ed.), *Routledge Handbook of Philosophy of Well-Being* (Routledge).
Heathwood, Chris (2013). 'Hedonism' in H. LaFollette (ed.), *International Encyclopedia of Ethics* (Wiley Blackwell).

Pleasure

Bramble, Ben (2013). 'The Distinctive Feeling Theory of Pleasure'. *Philosophical Studies*, 162(2): 201–217.
Bramble, Ben (2016). 'The Role of Pleasure in Well-Being' in G. Fletcher (ed.), *Routledge Handbook of Philosophy of Well-Being* (Routledge).

Gosling, Justin C. B. (1969). *Pleasure and Desire: The Case for Hedonism Reviewed* (Clarendon Press).

Experience machine objection

Baber, Harriet (2008). 'The Experience Machine Deconstructed'. *Philosophy in the Contemporary World*, 15(1): 133–138.

Hawkins, Jennifer (2016). 'The Experience Machine and the Experience Requirement' in G. Fletcher (ed.), *Routledge Handbook of Philosophy of Well-Being* (Routledge).

Hewitt, Sharon (2010). 'What Do Our Intuitions about the Experience Machine Really Tell Us about Hedonism?' *Philosophical Studies*, 151(3): 331–349.

Kawall, Jason (1999). 'The Experience Machine and Mental State Theories of Well-being'. *The Journal of Value Inquiry*, 33(3): 381–387.

Lin, Eden (forthcoming). 'How To Use The Experience Machine'. *Utilitas*.

Nagel, Thomas (1970). 'Death'. *Noûs*, 4(1): 73–80.

Nozick, Robert (1974). *Anarchy, State and Utopia* (Blackwell).

Weijers, Dan (2011). 'Intuitive Biases in Judgements about Thought Experiments: The Experience Machine Revisited'. *Philosophical Writings*, 50 & 51. http://danweijers.com/pdf/Intuitive%20Biases%20in%20Judgments%20about%20Thought%20Experiments%20(Dan%20Weijers).pdf, accessed 22 December 2015.

Qualitative hedonism

Fletcher, Guy (2008). 'The Consistency of Qualitative Hedonism and the Value of (at Least Some) Malicious Pleasures'. *Utilitas*, 20(4): 462–471.

Mill, J. S. (1863). *Utilitarianism* (Parker, Son, and Bourn).

Moore, G. E. (1903[2000]). *Principia Ethica*, Revised Edition, T. Baldwin (ed.) (Cambridge University Press).

Riley, Jonathan (1999). 'Is Qualitative Hedonism Incoherent?' *Utilitas*, 11(3): 347–358.

Saunders, Ben (2010). 'J. S. Mill's Conception of Utility'. *Utilitas*, 22(1): 52–69.

2 Desire-fulfilment theory

2.1 Introduction

In the previous chapter we examined hedonism. A common objection to hedonism is that we do not think that a person's well-being is determined solely by their hedonic level. We want to actually have certain kinds of relationships and achievements, not just the felt experience of having them. This thought leads naturally to the second major theory of well-being we are going to consider: the desire-fulfilment theory of prudential value (sometimes also called the 'desire-satisfaction theory of well-being'). In slogan form this theory says that getting what you want is good for you, not getting what you want is bad for you.

Before going into the details of the desire-fulfilment view it will be useful to get a general idea of it by seeing the answers that it would give in some cases. (For simplicity I assume that each agent in the example has only one desire):

Table 2.1

	Desire	*How the world is*
Annie	desires that her children are happy	Annie's children are happy
Noa	desires to be reading	Noa is reading
Allie	desires to have a boyfriend	Allie has a boyfriend
Caiden	desires to be 7ft tall	Caiden is only 6ft tall
Nilan	desires to be at home	Nilan is not at home
Marta	desires to be a zoologist	Marta is a tax lawyer

Taking the first three cases, the desire-fulfilment theory would hold that Annie's children being happy is good for Annie, that Noa's reading is good for Noa, and that Allie having a boyfriend is good for Allie. In every case this is true because these things *fulfil* the desires of the relevant person. By 'fulfil', I mean here simply that the world is the way that the person desires it to be (schematically: they desire that P and P is the case).

Moving to the second set of three cases, the desire-fulfilment theory would say that Caiden's being only 6ft tall is *bad* for Caiden, that Nilan's being at work is *bad* for Nilan, and Marta's being a tax lawyer is bad for Marta. In every case this is because these things *frustrate* (fail to fulfil) the desires of the relevant person. They desire the world to be a certain way and the world is *not* like that (they desire that P but *not-P* is the case).

Let us now look in more detail at the desire-fulfilment theory. We can formulate the theory more precisely as follows:

> DFT: Something is (non-instrumentally) good for you if and only if and because it fulfils a non-instrumental desire of yours. Something is (non-instrumentally) bad for you if and only if and because it frustrates a non-instrumental desire of yours.[1]

(Henceforth I often omit the 'non-instrumentally', for the sake of readability. All claims about what is good for should be taken to be about what is non-instrumentally good for, unless otherwise specified.)

To understand DFT fully we must be careful to note the following point. First, the formulation of DFT above had two 'and because' clauses. This is because DFT doesn't merely claim that anything that satisfies your desires is good for you (and vice versa). It claims something stronger than this. It claims that something's satisfying your desires *makes* it good for you. Take the example of a thermometer: It is 21 degrees outside if and only if an accurate thermometer says '21 degrees'. But the thermometer does not *make* it 21 degrees. By contrast, DFT ascribes to desires a special role in conferring prudential value. Desires *make* things good/bad for us.

This claim is important because it helps to make DFT a *distinct* theory of well-being. This is because a hedonist could argue as follows: 'It is true that all and only the things we desire are good for us. But this is only true because our desires reliably track what's independently good for us (namely pleasure).' If we formulate DFT simply as a bi-conditional (e.g. 'something is good for you if and only if it fulfils your desire') then the theory is compatible with hedonism, such that one could consistently hold both views. Thus for DFT to be a distinctive theory of well-being, and to understand the theory properly, we must keep in mind that it claims that something is good for someone *because* it fulfils their desire (or bad for them *because* it frustrates their desire).[2]

Second, DFT as formulated above makes reference to non-instrumental desires. Non-instrumental desires are desires that we have for things not solely on account of their further consequences. So, for example, suppose you desire money and you desire money solely in order to buy a house. In that case your desire for money is *instrumental*. You do not desire the money for its own sake or in and of itself but simply for the sake of what it would bring you. Conversely, suppose you desire to be a teacher. You do not desire to be a teacher for some further reason. Rather you simply desire to be a teacher for its own sake. In this case you have a non-instrumental desire. If, by contrast, you *also* desired to be a teacher in order to impress your parents then *that* desire would be an instrumental desire. The DFT's theory of what is non-instrumentally good for us is a claim about the connection between our well-being and what fulfils our non-instrumental desires.

Third, the DFT does not claim that you must *feel* fulfilled or even believe that your desire has been fulfilled for its fulfilment to be good for you. On DFT, it is good for you that the world is the way you desire it to be *whether you know this or not* and *whether you are thereby pleased.*

Here is an example. You are doing jury service during the World Cup. Your team, Costa Rica, are playing and you strongly desire that they win. But you are unable to watch the game and, because of restrictions on juror contact with the outside world, you have no access to the internet, TV or radio, etc. The game finishes at 5pm and, unbeknownst to you, Costa Rica won. Your juror deliberations continue right up until midnight when you are finally free to go and then, but only then, you hear the result. Between 5pm and midnight you desired that Costa Rica won the match. According to the desire-fulfilment theory of well-being your desire's being fulfilled – by Costa Rica winning the match – was good for you at 5pm even though you only knew of the fulfilment of this desire later.

To illustrate this point, note that DFT would say that if prior to midnight you had literally died of boredom during the juror deliberations and thus never learned the outcome of the game this wouldn't have prevented its being true that your desire had been satisfied (unbeknownst to you) and your well-being enhanced by Costa Rica winning the game.

Questions left open

Let me note some questions that my formulation and discussion of DFT leave open.

My formulation of DFT says nothing about the *nature* of desires, about what desires *are*. Further, DFT as formulated says nothing about how much prudential value results from the fulfilment of a desire. Different views are possible on this question. One view, perhaps the orthodox view, says that the prudential value of a desire-fulfilment is positively affected by features of the desire such as its *intensity*. On this view the fulfilment of a more intense desire is better for you than the fulfilment of a less intense desire. Another possible view says that *all* desire-fulfilments are equally good for the agent. I take no stand here on which of these developments of the view (if any) is (i) more plausible or (ii) more common. I will simply bracket those issues.[3]

DFT, as formulated above, also says nothing about how to balance what is good for you versus what is bad for you. Put another way, it does not tell us how your respective desire-fulfilments and frustrations serve to determine your *overall* level of well-being. These are all interesting issues that space precludes exploration of.

2.2 Arguments for DFT

I DFT can explain paradigm cases of prudential value

Take some paradigm cases of things that hold prudential value: having fun, spending time with friends, succeeding in one's goals. The desire-fulfilment theorist can plausibly say of each of these things that they are things that we *desire*. There is a strong correlation between things that are paradigmatically good for us and things that we desire. Thus some evidence for the DFT is the frequency with which we observe correlations between things that are good for an agent and things that they desire.

Relatedly, DFT can also appeal to some of the evidence that the hedonist uses to support their view. Remember this case

> **Raj on the Rollercoaster**: Raj is enjoying a rollercoaster ride. Suddenly, a bird flies into his face, which is very painful. After getting off the ride Raj is given some painkillers that numb the area and he feels no pain. His friend then buys him candy floss, which he loves, and pleasurably eats.

In this example it seems plausible that Raj's well-being level starts off fairly high, decreases suddenly, goes up a little, and then increases again a little later. DFT can point out that it is overwhelmingly plausible that as this case unfolds Raj has a desire-fulfilment (a desire to ride the rollercoaster, or a desire to experience pleasure, or both), then a desire-frustration (a desire not to be in pain), then a desire-fulfilment (a desire not to be in pain, which is fulfilled when he receives the painkiller). Finally he gets desire-fulfilment from the candy floss (a desire to eat candy floss, a desire for sugar, a desire for pleasure, or perhaps all three). Thus just as hedonism can plausibly claim a correlation between Raj's well-being and his hedonic level the DFT proponent can plausibly claim a correlation between Raj's well-being and his desire-fulfilments/frustrations.[4]

You might remember from the previous chapter the claim that a correlation between two things can be explained by a common third factor. The DFT can claim that desire-fulfilment is the third factor that explains the correlation between hedonic level and well-being. They will argue that hedonic level correlates with level of well-being because they both correlate with desire-fulfilments. They each correlate with desire-fulfilments because desire-fulfilment is what fundamentally matters to well-being and because we have desires for pleasure and to avoid pain.

In these ways DFT theorists can use as evidence for their view the plausible correlation between paradigmatic cases of an agent's well-being increasing or decreasing and their desires being satisfied.

2 DFT avoids experience machine objections

Hedonism is vulnerable to the experience machine objection because it gives no fundamental prudential importance to anything other than hedonic level. According to hedonism, any two agents with the same hedonic level have the same level of well-being whatever else might be true of each agent (even if one is having real experiences whilst the other is plugged into a machine having fake experiences). By contrast, the DFT is less vulnerable to the experience machine cases. This is because it gives fundamental importance to whether the world is actually how the agent desires it to be (and not simply to whether the agent has the experience as if their desires have been satisfied). Having the experience of your desire being satisfied (i.e. its seeming to you that your desire is satisfied) is distinct from its actually being satisfied. For this reason, the experience machine will say that an agent who wants to write a novel and have friends and be successful in her career is not benefitted by merely having the experience of this (no matter how convincing the experience). To see this compare these three cases:

Table 2.2

	Desires	*How the world is*	*Agent's experience*
Annie	her children are happy	her children are happy	her children are happy
Beryl	her children are happy	her children are happy	her children are not happy
Donald	to be a successful novelist	he isn't a successful novelist	he is a successful novelist

What does DFT say about these cases? It will say that both Annie and Beryl are benefitted by their desire being satisfied (even though Beryl has *misleading* evidence that her desire is not satisfied). Donald desires to be a successful novelist and in fact is not. So his desire is not satisfied and so this is bad for him. According to DFT, Donald's mistaken impression that he is a successful novelist is irrelevant; his desire to be a successful novelist is unsatisfied.

A common response at this point is as follows: 'Donald's desire *is* satisfied. He has the *impression* of being a successful novelist.' This is a mistake. Donald's desire is *to be a successful novelist*. His desire does not mention having the *experience* of being a successful novelist. Granted, in a more typical case Donald will have two desires (i) to be a successful novelist (ii) to have the experience of being a successful novelist and if that were so then one of his desires is satisfied.[5] But that does not change the verdict DFT is committed to in the case where Donald desires, simply, to be a successful novelist. His desire is unsatisfied in that case, irrespective of his misleading experience.

Desire-fulfilment theory nicely avoids the experience machine objection to hedonism precisely *because* it makes our well-being depend fundamentally on the world being the way we want it to be, on our getting what we want, rather than simply on the hedonic quality of our experience. What other arguments are there for desire-fulfilment theory?

3 Attitude-dependence

One consideration often appealed to in support of DFT is that it makes prudential value attitude-dependent in an appealing way. It is often thought that *prudential* value must be in some way sensitive to what we are like as individual agents and that, by focusing on our desires, DFT captures this sensitivity to what we are like.

As stated, this attitude-dependence criterion is vague. It is unclear both how strongly it supports DFT and how hard it would be for other theories to accommodate it.[6] But there does seem something plausible in the idea that prudential value requires the agent's endorsement or engagement in some way. DFT makes this endorsement or engagement very strong. This is because DFT holds each of the following:

i   You *must* desire X for X to be good for you [desire is necessary for prudential value].
ii   If you desire X then X is good for you [desire is sufficient for prudential value].

Thus if it is a good feature of a theory of well-being that it makes what is good for you sensitive to your attitudes, DFT seems to be well supported. It gives a very significant role to a person's attitudes in generating prudential value for them. (For much more detailed discussion of this see the appendix in chapter 3 titled 'Alienation and attitude-dependence'.)

4 Reason and motivation arguments

What else might one offer in support of DFT? One might argue as follows:

1   We always have some reason to do what is good for us.
2   We only have reason to A if we have a desire that is satisfied by A-ing.

Therefore,

3   Everything that is good for us satisfies one of our desires.

Therefore,

4   DFT is true.[7]

This is a neat argument. Premise (1) is very plausible. It does not say we always have sufficient or overall reason to do what is good for us. It says only that we always have *some* reason to do what is good for us. Premise (2) is a substantive view about reasons so it is a premise that some will reject. There is not sufficient space to assess premise (2) here, given that the question of when an agent has a reason to do something is a huge issue. A more local weak point in the argument is the transition from (3) to (4). It is easy to think that the gap between (3) and (4) is quite trivial, that once (3) is true then DFT simply must be true. But this would be a mistake. (3) claims only that it is true of everything that it is good for us that it fulfils one of our desires. But that could be true whilst the DFT is false.

To see why, suppose that hedonism is true. If hedonism plus premise (3) is a consistent set then (3) cannot entail (4) (given the assumption that DFT and hedonism cannot both be true). Is there a way for hedonism to be true along with premise (3)? Yes. This could be true for either, or both, of the following reasons: First, it might be true that all agents desire pleasure. Second, it might be true that all agents desire *what is good for them*. Taking the latter case, if all agents have the desire <*to get things that are good for me*> then anything that is good for them is something that fulfils this desire. So if hedonism is true all pleasures will be good for agents and, in virtue of being good for agents, will fulfil their desire for *what is good for me*. Thus, (1)–(3) are consistently combinable with hedonism and so (1)–(3) do not entail DFT.

The problem with the argument was the jump from (3) to (4). (3) claims that everything that has prudential value fulfils a desire of the agent. But that can be true just if the agent has some desire that is fulfilled by the things that are good for them, including the very general desire *to get things that are good for me*. Thus the problem is that (3) does not entail that things are good for us *because* they fulfil our desires and this is what would have to be true for DFT to be true.

Remember the point I made above in introducing DFT, that DFT doesn't merely claim that anything that satisfies your desires is good for you (and vice versa). It claims something stronger than this. It claims that something's satisfying your desires *makes* it good for you. Because DFT is committed to the claim that desires make things good/bad for us the jump from (3) to (4) is invalid. Even if everything that is good for us is something that we desire, that does not (by itself) mean that things are good for us because we desire them.

Having considered some of the arguments for DFT, let us look at some objections to the view.

2.3 Objections to DFT

The objections to DFT that we will examine here are all counterexamples based on the theory's implications in particular cases. The objections all work by highlighting apparent consequences of the view and arguing that these consequences cast doubt on the view. Thus the general form of these objections is:

1   If DFT is true then P is true.
2   P is not true.

Thus,

3   DFT is not true.

I will now run through some of the examples given of problematic conclusions that would follow from DFT.

> **The Stranger on a Plane**: On a plane from London to Madrid, Lucy meets Ben who tells her that he's going to a remote village in Spain to marry his childhood sweetheart, John. Lucy leaves the plane desiring that Ben is successful in this and that he lives a happy life. This happens but Lucy never hears from them and never travels near there again (nor do they ever visit England).

What must DFT say about this case? Lucy's desire is non-instrumental, it was the desire simply that Ben is successful in marrying John and living happily thereafter. And this event occurred. So the desire was satisfied. DFT must say that the fulfilment of this desire is, itself, good for Lucy. Put another way, DFT must say that there is prudential value for Lucy simply in virtue of Ben marrying John and being happy. But that seems implausible. Lucy has no clue that her desire is satisfied. She does not derive pleasure, or feel contentment that it is satisfied. She experiences no joy from the fact that Ben lives happily ever after. One might say that it is not a desire whose fulfilment makes any real difference to how her life goes.[8]

Here is another such case:

> **Life on Mars**: In 2014, Hilary desires that there is life elsewhere in the universe. Unbeknownst to all humans (and only discovered after her death) there is life on Mars in 2014.

What must DFT say about this case? Hilary's desire is non-instrumental, it is simply the desire *that there is life elsewhere in the universe.* And this was in fact the case, so the desire is satisfied. Clearly, the view says that the fulfilment of this desire is, itself, good for Hilary. Put another way, DFT must say that there is prudential value for Hilary simply in virtue of there being life elsewhere in the universe. But that seems implausible.

> **Stockholm Syndrome**: Phil is in a physically and psychologically abusive relationship. In time he stops desiring to leave his partner and his strongest

desire is simply to always remain with his partner. His few remaining friends and his doctor, aware of his situation, give him opportunities to escape but he declines.[9]

What must DFT say about this case? Phil's desire is non-instrumental, it is simply the desire to remain with his partner. And this was in fact the case, so the desire is satisfied. Clearly, DFT must say that the fulfilment of this desire is, itself, good for Phil. Put another way, DFT must say that there is prudential value for Phil simply in virtue of remaining with his partner. But that seems implausible.

These cases are typical cases of objections to DFT because it does not seem very plausible that, in and of themselves, the fulfilments of these desires are good for the relevant agents. So what can a DFT theorist say when presented with these cases?[10]

2.4 Replies to objections (1): biting the bullet

What can the DFT say in reply to the three kinds of counterexamples presented above? One strategy is to refine the view so as to avoid having the problematic implications highlighted in the examples. Thus when presented with the argument:

1   If DFT is true then P is true.
2   P is not true.

Therefore,

3   DFT is not true.

the DFT theorist can respond by trying to block premise (1), by altering the theory to prevent its entailing P. We will examine that strategy below. However, in *this* section we will examine a different strategy, one that concedes the first premise of the argument – and so concedes that DFT has the implications identified in the counterexample, but that denies premise (2), by denying that these implications are problematic. This response I will refer to as 'biting the bullet'.

How can DFT theorists bite the bullet on these three examples? Well, there are a number of different things that they can say. First, they might rightly point out that things that are good for someone to some *small* extent are easy to overlook, that it is easy to think that something is of *no* prudential value when, in fact, it is good for the agent but just not *very* good for them.[11] They might also then point out that it is useful to distinguish between (i) something's being good for someone to *some* extent and (ii) something's being in someone's *best* interests.[12] For example, the night before an important exam it might be good for you to go and have fun. But that might not be what is *best* for you, what would maximise your well-being (which would be to study or get a decent amount of sleep).

Taking the particular cases, the DFT theorist might claim that Lucy's and Hilary's lives *do* go better for them in virtue of their desire being satisfied. It might not make a big difference. But they are slightly higher in well-being and our tendency to judge otherwise (i.e. to judge that this desire-fulfilment has no prudential value for her) simply reflects a tendency to overlook small benefits.

In the case of Phil, the DFT theorist can argue that our judgement that his desire-fulfilment has no prudential value simply reflects our judgement that the fulfilment of this particular desire is not what leads to his greatest *overall* well-being. The DFT theorist can argue that it is not in Phil's *best* interests for this desire to stay with his partner to be satisfied – because if he were to leave this partner he would experience greater desire-fulfilment – but that this does not mean that the fulfilment of this desire has zero prudential value.

One feature of these responses is that they make assumptions about the nature of the desires in the examples. The responses depend on the claim that the fulfilment of these desires was only a *small*, easily overlooked, benefit. This might be the case if the agent has many other desires, desires not satisfied by the happy marriage, life on Mars, or staying with the partner (in the respective examples). But, taking just Hilary's case, could there not be a version of the case where Hilary desires *only* that there be life on Mars? Or, if the strength of a desire can affect the degree of prudential value its fulfilment would have, imagine that Hilary has other desires but that her desire that there be life on Mars is *much* stronger than her other desires. In either of these possible situations there seems no way for the DFT theorist to hold that the fulfilment of this desire is only a small benefit. Either it's Hilary's *only* desire or it's her strongest desire by some distance. If so, then it looks like the DFT would have to say that in this case the fulfilment of this desire would be a *significant* benefit.

The upshot of this is that the DFT needs to convince us that when we think about these alternate cases, ones where either (i) the desire in question is the agent's only desire, or (ii) by far their strongest desire, this makes it plausible that the fulfilment of the desire would actually be good for the agent, in and of itself.

Some might find this intuitive. They might agree with the DFT theorist that in the original versions of these cases we were mistakenly overlooking small benefits in judging that the desire-fulfilments were not good for the agent and that in these altered versions of the cases it is plausible that the fulfilments of these desires is actually good for the agent.

Some, however, will likely remain unconvinced. They might put forth their objection by saying that the mere fact of there being life on Mars just is not the right kind of thing to contribute to Hilary's well-being, that Ben happily marrying his childhood sweetheart is not the right kind of thing to hold prudential value for *Lucy* (absent her awareness of it or taking pleasure in it), or that Phil's desire is for something that just is *not* good for him, however strongly he desires it.

Having considered ways that the DFT can try to bite the bullet in the face of the counterexamples, let us now look at *another* way that the DFT can respond to counterexamples, by refining their view.

2.5 Replies to objections (2): refining the view

Remember the general schema of the objections to DFT:

1   If DFT is true then P is true.
2   P is not true.

Thus,

3   DFT is not true.

Cases like Lucy, Hilary and Phil work by pointing to desires whose fulfilment intuitively does not have prudential value for the agent. According to the DFT as formulated above there could not be any desires whose fulfilment does not have prudential value for the agent. In the previous section we saw how DFT theorists could argue that the fulfilment of the desires in question really is good for the agent, even if our initial judgement was otherwise. These were ways of *denying* premise (2).

An alternative strategy, the subject of this section, is for the DFT theorist to change the theory in a way that makes premise (1) not true for the revised theory. (Note, this strategy is not meant to help with all three problem cases, only the case of Phil.)

By far the most common way to revise the DFT is to change the focus of the theory away from fulfilment of the *actual* desires of the agent to the fulfilment of the desires they would have in some idealised or better circumstances. This is usually referred to as the desires of their idealised counterpart. There are many different questions that arise from this move. Here are just two:

1   What are the relevant idealising conditions? What makes the agent's counterpart *ideal*?
2   Does the view ascribe prudential value to the fulfilment of *all* of the idealised counterpart's desires? (This is how this kind of view is standardly understood. But note that one alternative is to hold that only the fulfilment of those desires of the actual agent that would be shared by their idealised counterpart have prudential value.)

Given the many different answers that could be given on question (1) and the possibility of different answers to (2), it would be misleading to refer to *the* ideal desire-fulfilment theory. For that reason I will often refer to ideal desire-fulfilment theor*ies* (IDFTs). However, for the sake of helping you to understand the difference between DFT and IDFTs, let me formulate a highly generic form of IDFT as follows:

> **IDFT 1**: something is non-instrumentally good for someone if and only if and because it fulfils the desires that they would have in ideal circumstances C (or that their idealised counterpart would have in C).

The most important question for IDFTs is: What are the idealising conditions? Here the IDFT theorist must give some indication as to what the relevant conditions are. If they do not then 'ideal circumstances C' would just function as a placeholder or 'black box' that generates no testable implications.

When spelling out the ideal circumstances, the IDFT theorist must do this in a way that (i) avoids the kinds of counterexamples that motivated moving to IDFT without (ii) generating equally bad problems for the view elsewhere. It is common for the IDFT theorist to claim that among the idealising conditions are:

1   The agent is instrumentally rational (they intend to take the means that maximise their ends as a whole).
2   The agent has full information about the possible objects of their desire.

Suppose that (1) and (2) are the IDFTs conception of ideal conditions. We can then formulate a particular version of IDFT thus:

> **IDFT 2**: something is non-instrumentally good for someone if and only if and because it fulfils the desires that they would have if they were instrumentally rational and had full information about the possible objects of desire.

Does moving from DFT to IDFT2 help to get around the cases above? It is not clear that it does.

Someone defending IDFT2 might argue that Phil's desire to stay with his partner is not one whose fulfilment would have prudential value for him because his desire manifests a failure of either instrumental rationality (perhaps staying with his partner leads to less desire-fulfilment *overall* than if he left them) or a lack of information that informs his desires (perhaps he does not properly understand the nature of his relationship or of what it would be like to leave it behind).

For this response to work it must be the case that Phil desires to stay with his partner only due to a failure of his practical rationality or through being insufficiently informed about the object of his desire. That will be a plausible diagnosis of many cases of problematic desires like Phil's.

However, a possible problem now appears: is it true that all problematic desires such as Phil's would be absent in the counterfactual condition (where he is fully informed and instrumentally rational)? Here is one reason to doubt that. Suppose that Phil has this unfortunate desire – to stay with his abusive partner – because years of abuse have left him with no confidence and no sense of self-worth, such that he thinks that he does not deserve anything good. Would this unfortunate condition definitely be rectified by his being fully instrumentally rational and fully informed about his options? It is not clear that that is so. In the absence of a reason to think that the addition of full information and instrumental rationality would have this transformative effect on Phil's desires, even the IDFT2 theorist might be forced to concede that the fulfilment of Phil's desire would be good for him.

The question of whether Phil's problematic desire would be absent in the idealising conditions is a general instance of a more general worry with the move to an idealised form of DFT such as IDFT: just what would agents desire in the condition of having full information?

Part of this worry is epistemological. Do we really *know* what agents would desire in these quite exotic conditions? If not, then it looks like IDFT2 leads quickly to a kind of scepticism about our knowledge of prudential value. Namely that we could not know what is good for people.[13]

A different worry concerns the possible causal *effects* of having full information. Perhaps knowing so much about the possible objects of desire would be thoroughly depressing. And how do we know that agents would not form all kinds of strange or destructive desires when put in that situation? This seems at least *possible* and for that reason the IDFT faces the worries that it might generate implausible results about what is good for agents, desires based on the problematic results of being an idealised agent.

The IDFT needs to supply a reason for optimism to counter the plausible observation that we possibly know very little about what it would be like to have this kind of full information and what desires would be formed under those conditions. We need some reasons to think (i) that we could know what desires would be formed in the idealising conditions (otherwise we end up with a form of scepticism) and (ii) that the desires formed in such a situation would plausibly generate prudential value for the agent.

So far we have examined possible problems for IDFT that stem from the possibility that the idealised agent's desires might be problematic because the addition of full information might either fail to rid the agent of their problematic desire or might generate new problematic desires.

Remember that the move from DFT to IDFT was designed to get around cases where it seemed implausible that satisfying the agent's actual desires would be good for them. A new worry for the IDFT stems from the observation that in shifting from the agent's actual desires to their idealised counterpart's the theory will lose its ability to get the right result in *un*problematic cases. Here's an example to demonstrate the worry:

Table 2.3

	Actual Joan	Idealised Joan
Desires	to attend the Super Bowl	to attend opera

(Here I have, artificially, just given each agent *one* desire, to make the example simple.)

Actual Joan strongly desires to attend the Super Bowl and it is plausible that the fulfilment of this desire would be good for Joan. Idealised Joan, by contrast, thinks football is boring and would *hate* to attend a match, much preferring the subtle complexities of the opera. Actual Joan *hates* the idea of the opera, finding it incomprehensible and boring.

IDFT says that it is *idealised* Joan's desires that determine what is good for Joan. In this case that generates the problematic result that there is prudential value for actual Joan in watching opera, even though this is something that actual Joan would find boring.

This problem, of divergence between Joan and idealised Joan's desires, is an instance of a more general problem for the IDFT. As mentioned above (§2 (3)), one of the motivations for desire-fulfilment theories of well-being is the thought that it nicely accommodates the way in which prudential value is in some way sensitive to what that agent is like. The move to IDFT risks making an agent's well-being sensitive not to what *that agent* is like but, rather, to what some idealised *counterpart* of that agent is like. And, as we have seen, to deal with some of the problematic desires that agents actually have, we have to allow quite a lot of difference between the idealised agent and the actual agent, in terms of their psychology and access to information. But once we allow the agents to diverge in these ways then it becomes increasingly unlikely that their desires will overlap. And the greater the degree of divergence in their desires, the less plausible it is to claim that DFT makes prudential value sensitive to what that agent is like.

Many are attracted to desire-fulfilment theories because they find it implausible that something could be non-instrumentally good for S even though S does not care about that thing *at all*. But IDFT2 leaves open this possibility, by allowing things that the actual agent does not care about to be good for them (in virtue of the desires of some idealised counterpart).

To help to understand the big picture, it might be useful to put these problems for IDFT together. Suppose we start with:

Actual Agent [desires: x, y, z, p1, p2, p3]

some of actual agent's desires are plausibly prudential value conferring (x, y, z) whilst others of actual agent's desires are problematic (the p desires). The problematic desires generate counterexamples to DFT. In response to such cases, the IDFTs suggest that we focus on an *idealised* agent's desires. We then need to find the right degree of idealisation. If the idealisation is too weak, so the agent is much like the actual agent, then the problematic desires, or some subset of them, might remain:

Weakly Idealised Agent [desires: x, y, z, p1, p2]

Alternatively, suppose that IDFT recommends focusing on the desires of a *highly* idealised agent. For all we know, a highly idealised agent might have one of the following desire sets:

Highly Idealised Agent1 [desires: p4, p5, p6]
Highly Idealised Agent2 [desires: a, b, c, d]

The trouble with highly idealised agent 1 is that they have problematic desires (their problematic desires are new ones, generated by the idealising features). Alternatively, as in highly idealised agent 2, it might be that there are no problematic desires but there are also no desires in common between the actual agent and their idealised counterpart. In this case the theory loses one of the DFT's main purported selling points – that it makes prudential value sensitive to what a person is like.

What is the upshot of all of this? Those tempted to respond to cases of problematic desires by moving from DFT to IDFT need to think carefully about the relevant idealising conditions. The idealising conditions must prevent problematic desires from being relevant to the actual agent's well-being. But at the same time the more greatly idealised the counterpart is the less able the IDFT is to accommodate the idea that it makes prudential value sensitive to what the person is actually like.[14]

2.6 The scope problem

Whatever success or failure IDFT enjoys with respect to problematic desires like Phil's, IDFT is no improvement with respect to the other two problem cases above, those of Lucy's and Hilary's desires. Lucy's desire was that some other person be happy, Hilary's desire was that there be intelligent life elsewhere in the universe. The problem for DFT was that it was implausible that the fulfilment of those desires *as such* (and whether or not the agent knows of their fulfilment) would be good for the agent. The problem these kinds of cases present to DFT is sometimes called the 'scope problem', the idea being that the scope of our desires is much wider than the set of things that plausibly hold prudential value for us.

By itself the move from DFT to IDFTs does not help with the scope problem.[15] Further, the scope problem might even be *worse* for the IDFT theorist. This will be the case if the more we learn about other people the more desires we would form about *their* lives. For example, if I know just how much some (hitherto-unknown) distant stranger desires a trip to the theme park, or a new job, or a child, that will likely make me desire that they get what they want.

Because each of DFT and IDFT will have to deal with the scope problem I will talk in terms of desire-fulfilment theories, where this is supposed to include idealising forms of the view. The scope problem for desire-fulfilment theories has not been solved.

To get a handle on what an adequate solution to the scope problem would be like, it will be useful to start with an obviously problematic proposal. Suppose that the desire-fulfilment theorist amended their theory as follows:

> **Self-interested desire-fulfilment theory:** Something is non-instrumentally good for you if and only if and because it fulfils a self-interested, non-instrumental, desire of yours. Something is non-instrumentally bad for you if and only if and because it frustrates a self-interested, non-instrumental, desire of yours.

What is wrong with this proposal? The answer is that it is circular and unilluminating. Remember that the original scope problem arises from our judgement that some desire-fulfilments are irrelevant to the well-being of the agent. The task for the proponent of DFT is therefore to try to filter those problem cases out, by telling us how those desires differ from the ones that look like they are candidates for affecting the agent's well-being. By reformulating the view in terms of 'self-interested' desires, this proposal simply assumes the distinction that we are trying to draw, rather than providing it. So whilst the proposal would certainly get the right answers about prudential value in particular cases, it does not help us to understand *how* those right answers come to be generated.

In light of the failure of the previous proposal we can see that the DFT solution to the scope problem has to be one that provides a genuine *explanation* of the difference between (a) desire-fulfilments that add to well-being and (b) those that do not.

Let us look at a second possible proposal for solving the scope problem. Suppose that the desire-fulfilment theorist amended their theory as follows:

> **Experiential Desire-Fulfilment Theory:** Something is non-instrumentally good for you if and only if and because it fulfils a non-instrumental, *experiential*, desire of yours. Something is non-instrumentally bad for you if and only if and because it frustrates a non-instrumental, experiential, desire of yours.

An experiential desire is a desire for a kind of experience. The desire *to experience being a successful novelist* is a desire for a particular kind of experience and so an experiential desire. By contrast the desire *to be a successful novelist* is simply a desire that one's novels be excellent and well-received (which may be the case without one knowing it) and not an experiential desire.

How does this proposal compare with the previous one? Well, it improves upon it in actually trying to articulate the distinction between desire-fulfilments relevant to an agent's well-being and those that are not relevant to it. The problem with it is that it is *too* restrictive, it makes too few desire-fulfilments relevant to the agent's well-being. Those attracted to DFT will likely baulk at the idea that only experiential desire-fulfilments can contribute to the agent's well-being. Furthermore, if the only desires that are relevant to an agent's well-being are desires for particular experiences then the DFT loses one of its key advantages over hedonism in avoiding the experience machine objection. For these reasons let us assume that desire-fulfilment theorists should not move from DFT to Experiential Desire-Fulfilment Theory.

Let us consider a third proposal. Suppose that the desire-fulfilment theorist amended their theory as follows:

> **Existence-Entailing Desire-Fulfilment Theory:** Something is non-instrumentally good for you if and only if and because it fulfils a non-instrumental, *existence-entailing*, desire of yours. Something is non-instrumentally bad for you if and only if and because it frustrates a non-instrumental, *existence-entailing*, desire of yours.

An existence-entailing desire is a desire whose fulfilment entails the existence of the agent whose desire it is. For example, my desire *to be famous during my lifetime* is existence-entailing. The desire cannot be fulfilled if I am dead. By contrast, the desire *for posthumous fame* is not existence-entailing as this desire can be fulfilled if I am dead.[16] Another desire that is not existence-entailing is the desire *that Tottenham win the Champions League*. That desire can be fulfilled even if I am dead.

How does this proposal compare with the previous ones? It provides a clear way of distinguishing the well-being-relevant desire-fulfilments from those that are not. It is therefore explanatory. And narrowing down to the class of desires whose fulfilments require the existence of the agent is less restrictive than narrowing down to desires for particular experiences. Further, focusing on the class of existence-entailing desires also does not undermine the ability of the view to avoid experience machine problems. Going back to the problem cases that generated the scope problem, this third proposal does seem to give plausible answers. Taking the examples of Lucy and Hilary, it says that the fulfilment of their desires cannot, by itself, hold prudential value for them.

At first pass, this is the best proposal of the three we have considered. Why might DFT theorists still have qualms about the view? I think the main source of doubt will be that Existence-Entailing Desire-Fulfilment Theory (EEDFT) is *too* restrictive.[17]

EEDFT does rule out some examples of desire-fulfilments that some will want to categorise as prudential value conferring. Those tempted by desire-fulfilment theories in general are likely to think that there are at least some desires that are not existence-entailing but whose fulfilment would be good for the agent. For example, suppose I desire *that my child is happy*. This is not existence-entailing. So according to EEDFT the fulfilment of this desire does not contribute to my well-being. Some of those who are otherwise attracted to DFT will baulk at this.

Another aspect of the restriction generated by Existence-Entailing Desire-Fulfilment Theory is that it rules out posthumous benefits and harms. This is because for obvious reasons nothing after the agent's death can be an existence-entailing desire-fulfilment. For example, if I desire *that climate change be stopped* the occurrence of this event after my death cannot possibly be good for me, according to EEDFT. Some will find this result completely fine and intuitive. We will look at posthumous harms and benefits in a later chapter so I will not go into more detail here. All that is important for now is seeing why *some* who would be attracted to desire-fulfilment theories in general will be uneasy about solving the scope problem by adopting EEDFT.

I claimed above that the scope problem has not yet been solved. We have examined only three possible proposals but their strengths and weaknesses give an idea of what the desire-fulfilment theorist needs in order to solve the scope problem.

2.7 Filtering desires? Tracking?

In this chapter we started off with DFT and then we looked at a number of different developments of the view. An important feature of desire-fulfilment theories, one worth reiterating, is that they claim that things are good for agents because they satisfy their desires. We spent much of this chapter looking at ways of developing DFTs to get around objections. Each development was designed to get around the same kind of problem for DFT: problematic desires, cases where a desire-fulfilment seems not to plausibly add to the agent's well-being. One kind of development of DFT was to idealise the relevant agent. Another was to try to solve the scope problem. The attempted solutions all worked by restricting the desires to filter out desires for remote things and focus instead on desires whose fulfilments are plausibly connected to the agent's well-being.

At some point in the preceding discussions you will likely have had the following worry: If the desire-fulfilment theorist thinks that desires *make* things good for us, what justification is there for restricting the agent's desires at all? Why can only *some* of the agent's desires bestow prudential value and not all of them if, as is claimed, things have prudential value **because** they fulfil the agent's desires?

This gets to the heart of a tricky issue for DFT in dealing with the kind of problems we have examined in this chapter. They need to solve the scope problem (among others) but they must do so without leaving themselves open to the objection that they are making desires merely *track* prudential value, rather than create it. To put it another way, someone might object to the DFT theorist that these attempts to find the *privileged* set of desires undermines the DFT theory by reflecting the fact that, in fact, desires do not create prudential value. Rather, it is simply that *some* of our desires happen to be for things that are good for us (whether we desire them or not). In thinking about the plausibility of the desire-fulfilment theory, and how it can be developed, one must thus try to steer a course between the following two considerations:

1   For DFT to be a genuine theory of well-being it must be that the agent's desires, or the relevant subset of their desires, really play a role in generating prudential value and do not merely happen to be desires for things that are, desire-independently, good for them.
2   At least some of an agent's actual desires do not seem to be desires whose fulfilment would necessarily be good for the agent.

2.8 Conclusion

In this chapter we have examined desire-fulfilment theories of well-being. They claim that an agent's desires (either the actual agent, or some idealised counterpart of the agent) confer prudential value. More specifically, they claim that the things are non-instrumentally good for the agent if and only if and because they satisfy the relevant agent's desires. The main challenge to DFTs was the numerous instances where it did not seem plausible that simply desiring some outcome would, by itself, make that desire's being satisfied good for the agent. A residual worry was that in attempting to reply to these kinds of cases, DFTs left themselves open to the charge that, really, desires are reliable *trackers* of prudential value rather than creators of it.

Comprehension questions

1   Which of the following claims is compatible with hedonism and why?

    i   Something is good for us if and only if we desire it.
    ii   All and only the things we desire are good for us.

2   If DFT is true are we *infallible* with respect to our own well-being? If so, why? If not, why not?
3   Are desire-fulfilment theories vulnerable to experience machine objections? If so, why? If not, why not?

Further questions

1   Suppose that a person desires to be badly off. Is that possible, if the desire-fulfilment theory is true?

2   Can a person successfully act upon the desire *to help someone else* without benefitting themselves? If so, how? If not, is this a problem?
3   Can we formulate an analogue of the base pleasures *equality* objection against DFT? If so, how? What should a DFT theorist say in response?

Notes

1   I am assuming that DFT is best formulated in terms of non-instrumental desires. But, like many other aspects of DFT, this is up for debate. One might argue that the view is better formulated in terms of some other set of desires.
2   There are actually two ways of understanding DFT. The first, which I am using, is that something – P – is good for you because you desire P. A second way of understanding DFT is as the claim that the combination of a-desire-for-P-and-P is what is good for you. If you do not see the difference do not worry. The difference between these two ways of formulating the view is (a) subtle and bears on some tricky issues elsewhere and (b) not important in this chapter (or the rest of the book). So you can safely ignore it here.
3   One other possibility is to give significance to the length of time that the desire was held.
4   Note: I say 'plausibly'. It may be that DFT actually cannot capture the correlation in every case. For arguments to this effect see Lin (2015).
5   One might reasonably think that the most realistic case is one where Donald desires *to have the experience of being a successful novelist because he is a successful novelist*.
6   See the appendix in chapter 3 titled 'Alienation and attitude-dependence'.
7   For discussion of related arguments see Heathwood (2016) and Lin (2015).
8   Those who think that there is an experience requirement on well-being (see previous chapter) will say that the problem is that the satisfaction of Lucy's desire has no impact upon her experience.
9   For discussion of these kinds of cases see Baber (2007), Nussbaum (2000).
10 Note that DFT in its standard form, as formulated above, must say not only (i) that Lucy, Hilary and Phil's desire-fulfilments are good for them but also (ii) that these desire-fulfilments are equally good for them as any other equal-sized desire-fulfilment (i.e. the fulfilment of any other equally intense desire). We could therefore mount an analogue of the base pleasures *equality* objection to attack DFT. Constraints of space preclude doing so here.
11 For further discussion of these issues, see e.g. Lukas (2010).
12 For further discussion of these issues, see e.g. Heathwood (2005).
13 For discussion, see Railton (1986).
14 Of course the IDFT theorist might reject the idea that prudential value is sensitive to what the actual agent is like. But this would be quite a costly move.
15 To be clear, the move from DFT to IDFT was not intended to get around cases like Lucy's desire and Hilary's desire, or the scope problem generally. The scope problem (which may be worse for the IDFT than the DFT theorist) is something that must be dealt with some other way.
16 More precisely, it is *non-existence*-entailing. It can only be fulfilled if I am dead.
17 For further discussion see Heathwood (2016).

References

DFT

Heathwood, Chris (2016). 'Desire-fulfillment theory' in G. Fletcher (ed.), *The Routledge Handbook of Philosophy of Well-Being* (Routledge).

DFT, reasons and motivation

Lin, Eden (2015). 'Prudence, Morality, and the Human Theory of Reasons'. *The Philosophical Quarterly*, 65(259): 220–240.

Objections to DFT

Baber, Harriet (2007). 'Adaptive Preference'. *Social Theory and Practice*, 33(1): 105–126.

Bradley, Ben (2007). 'A Paradox for Some Theories of Welfare'. *Philosophical Studies*, 133(1): 45–53.

Lauinger, William (2011). 'Dead Sea Apples and Desire-Fulfillment Welfare Theories'. *Utilitas*, 23(3): 324–343.

Lin, Eden (2015). 'The Subjective List Theory of Well-Being'. *Australasian Journal of Philosophy*, 1–16. http://doi.org/10.1080/00048402.2015.1014926, accessed 22 December 2015.

Nussbaum, Martha (2000). *Women and Human Development* (Cambridge University Press).

The scope problem

Hooker, Brad (1991). 'Marc Overvold's Contribution to Philosophy'. *Journal of Philosophical Research*, 16: 333–344.

Lukas, Mark (2010). 'Desire-Satisfactionism and the Problem of Irrelevant Desires'. *Journal of Ethics and Social Philosophy*, 4(2) (June): 1–24.

Overvold, Marc Carl (1980). 'Self-Interest and the Concept of Self-Sacrifice'. *Canadian Journal of Philosophy*, 10(1): 105–118.

Portmore, Douglas W. (2007). 'Welfare, Achievement, and Self-Sacrifice'. *Journal of Ethics and Social Philosophy*, 2(2): 1–28.

Rosati, Connie S. (2009). 'Self-Interest and Self-Sacrifice'. *Proceedings of the Aristotelian Society*, 109(1 pt3): 311–325.

Actual vs ideal desire-fulfilment

Enoch, David (2005). 'Why Idealize?' *Ethics*, 115(4): 759–787.

Heathwood, Chris (2005). 'The Problem of Defective Desires'. *Australasian Journal of Philosophy*, 83(4): 487–504.

Murphy, Mark C. (1999). 'The Simple Desire-Fulfillment Theory'. *Noûs*, 33(2): 247–272.

Railton, Peter (1986). 'Facts and Values'. *Philosophical Topics*, 14(2): 5–31.

Rosati, Connie S. (1995). 'Persons, Perspectives, and Full Information Accounts of the Good'. *Ethics*, 105(2): 296–325.

Rosati, Connie S. (1996). 'Internalism and the Good for a Person'. *Ethics*, 106(2): 297–326.

Sobel, David (2009). 'Subjectivism and Idealization'. *Ethics*, 119(2): 336–352.

Sophisticated developments of desire-fulfilment theories

Bykvist, Krister (2006). 'Prudence for Changing Selves'. *Utilitas*, 18(3): 264–283.

Dorsey, Dale (2013). 'Desire-Satisfaction and Welfare as Temporal'. *Ethical Theory and Moral Practice*, 16(1): 151–171.

Heathwood, Chris (2006). 'Desire Satisfactionism and Hedonism'. *Philosophical Studies*, 128(3): 539–563.
Rosati, Connie S. (1996). 'Internalism and the Good for a Person'. *Ethics*, 106(2): 297–326.

The nature of desire

Schroeder, Timothy (2006). 'Desire'. *Philosophy Compass*, 1(6): 631–639.
Schroeder, Timothy (2009). 'Desire'. *Stanford Encyclopedia of Philosophy*, 1(6): 631–639.

3   Objective list theories

3.1 Introduction

In the previous chapters we examined hedonism and desire-fulfilment theories. The main challenge to hedonism was the apparent implausibility of the claim that our hedonic levels are the only things that determine our level of well-being. For whilst it is plausible that many kinds of pleasure are (non-instrumentally) good for us, it seems implausible that absolutely nothing else is good for us.

The main challenges to desire-fulfilment theories were as follows. First, there are many actual and possible desires for things (such as life on Mars) that do not plausibly seem capable of being good for us (so desires do not have the power to make just anything prudentially valuable for us). Second, it seemed like there were some things that it would be good for someone to get even if the person himself does not desire them.

What might one conclude from these verdicts on hedonism and desire-fulfilment theory? One thing one might conclude is that hedonism is *partly* right because at least some pleasures are good for us but that at least some other things are good for us and are so independently of whether we desire them. This leads naturally to the class of objective list theories (OLTs) of well-being.

What an objective list theory claims

Unlike hedonism and the desire-fulfilment theory of well-being, it is difficult to characterise objective list theories in general. This is partly because, to a greater extent than is true for hedonism and the desire-fulfilment theory, 'objective list theory' names something from within a *very* wide *class* of theories. Nevertheless, there is one claim that objective list theories have in common. Such theories hold that at least some things are good for agents even if the agent does not desire them. (They also typically, though not always, hold that a *plurality* of things are non-instrumentally good for us, a complication we will revisit shortly.)

Let me now give a more precise characterisation of the core commitment of objective list theories. What objective list theories hold in common is the following claim about the independence of prudential value from desires:

> **Attitude-independence**: it is *not* the case that G is non-instrumentally good for S only if S desires G.[1]

This might seem a little unclear at first pass. To understand it better it will be useful to look at the claim that it is the negation of. The claim that the objective list theorist *rejects* is the following:

> **Attitude-dependence**: G is non-instrumentally good for S only if S desires G.[2]

(Henceforth I often omit the 'non-instrumentally', for the sake of readability. All claims about what is good for should be taken to be about what is non-instrumentally good for, unless otherwise specified.)

Attitude-dependence holds that a necessary condition of something being good for S is that S desires that thing. So, for example, virtue is good for S *only* on the condition that S desires virtue. And so on for all other goods. The objective list theorist denies attitude-dependence by denying that there is such a connection between well-being and desire.

By rejecting attitude-dependence and embracing attitude-independence, the objective list theorist allows that at least one good is good for an agent even if that agent does not desire that thing.

Attitude-independence is, I have just claimed, the heart of the objective list theory. But as mentioned above, a typical, but non-defining, feature of objective list theories is *pluralism*.[3] Objective list theories *typically* claim that more than one thing is non-instrumentally good for us. For example, they might claim that the following are all non-instrumentally good for us: pleasure, friendship, knowledge.

Pluralism is not, however, a *necessary* feature of an objective list theory. One could hold a *monistic* objective-list theory. This would be to hold (i) *attitude-independence* along with (ii) the claim that only one thing contributes positively to well-being. Here is an example of a monistic objective list theory, just to make the point clear:

> **Knowledgism**: All and only knowledge is the only prudential good.

Knowledgism is clearly monistic; it says that exactly one thing contributes positively to well-being. Knowledgism is also clearly attitude-independent. By holding that all knowledge has prudential value it claims that knowledge is good for an agent *whether they desire it or not*.[4]

We have seen that objective list theories are united in holding the attitude-independence claim. We have also seen that an objective list theory can either be monistic or pluralistic. What this helps us to see is that the category of 'objective list theories' is extremely wide. For that reason it is misleading to talk about *the* objective list theory.

Before looking at some more specific examples of objective list theories let me pause to briefly note two other features of objective list theories as a category.

First, objective list theories are theories of *prudential* value only. Thus it is not essential to an objective list theory to hold that the things on the list are valuable in some other, non-prudential, way also (such as being *morally* valuable). Of course an objective list theorist might *also* think that the goods on the list are morally valuable. But this is an additional, separate, commitment.

Second, objective list theories give no fundamental role to people's *beliefs* about what is good for them. Thus we are not free, according to the objective list theories, to 'devise our own lists'. An objective list theorist believes that the items on the list are all and only the things that are good for all humans.[5]

Questions left open

Let me note some issues that my characterisation of objective list theories has so far left open.

First, my formulation of OLT has said nothing about the *negative* side of well-being. However, it seems natural to assume that an objective list theorist of what is good for us would also accept attitude-independence for what is bad for us. Thus for the rest of this chapter I will assume that the objective list theorist accepts the following version of attitude-independence:

> **Attitude-independence***: it is not the case that G is non-instrumentally good (/bad) for S only if S desires G (/is averse to G).

Second, my formulation of OLT has said nothing about how, in the case of a pluralist OLT, the relative importance of the goods is determined. Of course there are *many* different possibilities. One could hold, for example, that all of the goods are equally important or one could give priority to some goods over others such that a life high in well-being must have a certain amount of one of the goods in particular. Given the range of possibilities, I will abstract from that issue in the discussion below.

It will be useful at some points in the discussion to have an example objective list theory to use to illustrate particular points. Let us work then with this exemplar objective list theory, which holds that the positive well-being contributors are pleasure, friendship and achievement. I will call this theory *three goods* for brevity.

3.2 Arguments for objective list theories

I Avoiding the experience machine problems

As we saw in a previous chapter, hedonism encounters difficulties with the experience machine. This is because hedonism holds that your hedonic level fully determines your level of well-being. Put another way, they are committed to the claim that nothing is non-instrumentally good and bad for you other than pleasure and pain. Cases like the experience machine cast doubt on this because they suggest that well-being is positively affected by other things, things such as achievement and friendship (as opposed to simply the pleasurable experience of having these things).

It is fairly simple to see how objective list theories have an advantage over hedonism with respect to the experience machine. The OL theorist can explain our sense that a life in the experience machine at hedonic level L need not have the same level of well-being as one outside the machine at hedonic level L as stemming from the fact that the two lives differ with respect to other, non-hedonic, goods.

Here is an example. Imagine some rich and successful life full of enjoyment, friendship and achievement (see Chapter 1). Then imagine a life plugged into the machine with the same experiential and hedonic qualities (but no real friendship or achievement). Suppose you think that the former life is higher in well-being than the latter. This can be easily explained by an objective list theory that counts achievement and friendship among the non-instrumental prudential values such as *three goods*. After all, on the *three goods* theory, the two lives have the following prudential profiles, respectively:

Not plugged in	*Plugged in*
Hedonic Level L	Hedonic Level L
Friendship	No Friendship
Achievement	No achievement

The non-plugged-in life contains achievement and friendship whereas the plugged-in life lacks these. It is thus straightforward for the *three goods* theory to provide a justification for thinking that the unplugged life is better than the plugged-in life. And the same kind of explanation will be available to other objective list theories.

2 Avoiding the scope problem

As argued in the previous chapter, desire-fulfilment theories (DFT) are vulnerable to a 'scope objection'. One example of this was the following case:

Life on Mars: In 2014, Hilary desires that there is life elsewhere in the universe. Unbeknownst to all humans (and only discovered after her death) there is life on Mars in 2014.

The problematic verdict that DFT is committed to in this case is that the fulfilment of this desire is, itself, good for Hilary. That is, it is good for Hilary simply that there is life elsewhere in the universe (whether or not she discovers this or knows it) because this fulfils her desire. The same went for other problematic cases such as:

> **The Stranger on a Plane**: On a plane from London to Madrid, Lucy meets Ben who tells her that he's going to a remote village in Spain to marry his childhood sweetheart, John. Lucy leaves the plane desiring that Ben is successful in this and that he lives a happy life. This happens but Lucy never hears from them and never travels near there again (nor do they ever visit England).

In specifying an exhaustive list of positive contributors to well-being and, specifically, by treating well-being as independent of an agent's attitudes, objective list theories are well placed to avoid this scope problem that arises for desire-fulfilment theories. For example, the *three goods* theory can explain why life elsewhere in the universe is not, itself, good for Hilary – and why John and Ben's marriage is not, itself, good for Lucy – by pointing out that these things are not instances of friendship or achievement. And the same kind of explanation will be available to other objective list theories.

3 Pre-theoretical judgements

The two arguments for objective list theories that we have seen so far are advantages that the view has in avoiding objections to two of its main competitors. Another, less reactive, advantage that OLT has is its according with our pre-theoretical judgements about well-being. If you ask people what they ultimately want for themselves and their loved ones they will typically give you a list of items – health, pleasure, friendship, knowledge, achievement – without thinking either that these can all be reduced to one value or that the list is simply determined by what their loved ones in fact desire.

Objective list theory is in this way analogous to common-sense morality in being a kind of widely held pre-theoretic view of well-being. It seems to function as the view that one holds before and until one is persuaded to adopt one of the other philosophical theories of well-being. Thus one ground that might be offered for holding an objective list theory is that it is supported by our pre-theoretic intuitive judgements about well-being, or the judgements that we make about well-being outside of, or before, philosophical thinking about the nature of well-being. That is to say, one might argue that our pre-theoretical judgements – judgements reflected in the prudential choices we make, the way that we give prudential advice, and the way that we care for family and friends – are some *evidence* in favour of objective list theories.

Reply

An objector to objective list theories might dispute this claim that our every-day pre-theoretical judgements provide support for objective list theories. One way that they might do this is by giving an account of why our everyday prudential judgements are actually better evidence for some *other* theory of well-being. Alternatively, perhaps more plausibly, the objector might concede that the *observation* is correct – that objective list is a common starting point and a widely held view among non-philosophers – but dispute the significance of this, arguing that it is only weak evidence (if any) of the truth of objective list theories.

One ground for such doubt might be the fact that it is *pre*-theoretic judgements that are being appealed to, where an opponent of an objective list theory might think that such judgements are naive or unlikely to be very important.

One way of casting doubt on the importance of matching our pre-theoretic judgements is to point out that people often seem inconsistent in the judgements they make about prudential value. For example, people often say that friendship and achievement belong on the list of well-being contributors but nonetheless also commonly claim that (in cases of deception) 'what you don't know won't hurt you', a slogan that is plausibly inconsistent with thinking that achievement or friendship themselves have prudential value (after all, you could be deceived about whether you have these goods).

A second way of casting doubt on the importance of pre-theoretic judgements is to note that non-philosophers often conflate instrumental and non-instrumental prudential value. For that reason it might be that the *pluralistic* nature of the accounts of well-being we are tempted to prior to philosophising about well-being reflects a failure to distinguish what is instrumentally good for us from what is non-instrumentally good for us. To give one example, one might claim that we tend to think that friendship has non-instrumental prudential value only because friendship is generally a rich source of pleasure. That is, we mistakenly think that the friendship itself is non-instrumentally good for us when really it is just (highly) instrumentally good for us.

4 Arguments from the details of particular theories

The three arguments given so far were mostly arguments for objective list theories in general. However it is worth noting that particular instances of objective list theories will also have their own particular merits. Thus one *type* of argument that will be possible for any particular OLT is to point out its plausible implications in actual and possible cases. Here are two examples to illustrate the point.

First, suppose one held an OLT that claims that *privacy* has prudential value. One argument that could be given in favour of such a view is that it nicely coheres with and justifies the view that people are harmed by their privacy being invaded (such as through their phone being hacked or their emails being monitored) whether or not they knew that this was taking place.

Second, an OLT that has autonomy on the list would be able to explain why we think that there are quite significant restrictions on the extent to which we can interfere in the lives of others (at least with respect to behaviour that does not harm others). This kind of restriction would be nicely explained by an OLT with autonomy on the list for then it would be the case that by interfering one undermines a person's autonomy and thus reduce their degree of this prudential good.

Those are just two examples but they demonstrate that particular objective list theories will have particular arguments in their favour.

3.3 Objections to objective list theories

Just as I finished the previous section by noting that many arguments for objective list theories will stem from their particular details, so too will many objections to particular objective list theories depend upon their specific details. In this section I will largely abstract from particular objective list theories and consider problems and objections that apply to such theories generally (even if to unequal extents).

I Arbitrariness and explanatory impotence

One kind of objection to objective list theories is the claim that the theories are problematically arbitrary, nothing but an 'unconnected heap', or somehow explanatorily unsatisfying.

One point that this objection draws attention to is the difference between two kinds of objective theories. The first claims that no explanation can be given for why any of the goods appear on the list. Borrowing the label from Philip Kitcher, let us call this a form of 'brute objectism'.[6] Another kind of objective list theory claims that there can be at least a partial, if not a complete, explanation of the presence of the goods on the list, an explanation of why these things are good for us. Following Kitcher (1999) again, let us call this 'explanatory objectivism'.

To see the difference between these two forms of objective theory, notice two claims that one could combine with the *three goods* theory:

Brute objectivism

  i   Pleasure, achievement, friendship have prudential value.
  ii There is no (non-trivial) explanation of why (i) is true.

Explanatory objectivism

  i   Pleasure, achievement, friendship have prudential value.
  ii There is at least some explanation of why (i) is true.

There are different degrees of explanation that can be offered by explanatory objectivists. At one end of the spectrum is a view that provides only a partial explanation of (i), by explaining why (e.g.) one of the particular goods has prudential value. At the other end of the spectrum are forms of explanatory objectivism that offer a *complete* explanation of (i), an explanation that explains for each item on the list why it is on the list.

The objection mentioned above, that objective list theories are problematically arbitrary, nothing but an 'unconnected heap', or somehow explanatorily unsatisfying, clearly varies in its relevance depending upon whether we are considering brute forms of objectivism or explanatory forms of objectivism in mind.

The most ambitious kinds of explanatory objectivism – ones that supply a complete explanation for the goods on the list – are immune to *this* objection. To give one such example, imagine one held that pleasure, achievement and friendship were the sole prudential values and that this is because they (and only they) constitute the exercise of our distinctively human nature.[7] This would be to supply a complete explanation of why these things are on the list. It thus avoids the charge of being ad hoc. That is *not* to say that simply by offering an explanation the explanatory objectivist is in the clear. It might be that the explanation it provides is *implausible*. But that is a different problem from not supplying an explanation.

Ben Bradley gives a succinct spelling-out of a cluster of related objections to objective list theories. He writes:

> [P]luralism seems objectionably arbitrary. Whatever the composition of the list, we can always ask: why should these things be on the list? What do they have in common? What is the rational principle that yields the results that these things, and no others, are the things that are good?[8]

Although Bradley couches this as an objection to 'pluralism', at least part of his objection(s) applies equally well to monistic objective list theories such as knowledgism. One reply the objective list theorist can make is that the objective list theory is no more burdened by these challenges than any other theory of well-being. We can ask: 'why is pleasure (or knowledge or...) alone of prudential value?' or 'what is the rational principle that determines that pleasure (or knowledge or...) contributes to well-being?'

We can also make the same charge against other theories of well-being. Desire-fulfilment theorists spend little or no time providing an *explanation* of *why* desire-fulfilment contributes to well-being. And the same goes for hedonism.

There are two good reasons to think that such fundamental questions are, at best, *extremely* difficult to answer. First, the *fundamental* truths about well-being are plausibly *necessary* truths. For that reason they may be *incapable* of further explanation. It might be that there is no further, non-trivial, explanation of why e.g. pleasure contributes to well-being (or why achievement does, or why friendship does...).

One might instead read Bradley's complaint as an epistemic one, a worry about how we could know that (e.g.) *three goods* is true. This is an understandable worry. Given that the fundamental tenets of a theory of well-being are *evaluative* truths – as opposed to purely descriptive truths about how the world *is* – at least part of the issue here is that we have no well-worked-out account of how knowledge is possible when it comes to evaluative matters. Thus, the objective list theorist might say, Bradley points out difficulties for the objective list theory but not difficulties peculiar to the objective list theory in particular. Rather the difficulty is one for all theories of well-being, namely that of explaining how we could know that they are true.

These replies have some merit. Note however that they really show only that all theories of well-being share the same *kinds* of challenges. But this leaves open the possibility that objective list theories (strictly speaking, *pluralistic* ones) have especially difficult instances of them. One reason for thinking this is that it has to provide an account of why *each* constituent good is a fundamental prudential value. Thus if we are comparing the costs of the theories of well-being it is a *pro tanto* cost of (pluralistic) objective list theories that they will need to provide a fundamental explanation of, or explanation of our knowledge of, more than one type of good. With respect to these issues, then, hedonism and desire-fulfilment enjoy an advantage over some forms of objective list theories (particularly brute ones and pluralistic ones) but are arguably tied with monistic objective list theories.

A final thread to Bradley's objection is a challenge to the (pluralist) objective list theorist to provide an explanation of the *commonality* between the items on the list. If the idea is that the objective list theorist must provide an explanation of why the items on the list have the common property of enhancing well-being then this is a restatement of the first objection. And the answers provided by the OLT will differ depending on whether they are brute objectivists or explanatory objectivists.

An alternative way of reading it is as a request for an explanation of what properties the items on the list have in common. Of course one answer that the objective list theorist is committed to is that the items on the list have the property of *enhancing well-being*. However, that is trivial so we must read the demand, instead, as one of asking what properties the items on the list have in common, aside from their contributing to well-being.

At this point the objective list theorist has options. They can either question the legitimacy of the demand by asking what reason we have to expect the items on the list will have some property in common aside from contributing to well-being. This response is most likely taken by the brute objectivist. Another, more positive, strategy is simply to note that the items on any plausible objective list will have points of commonality. For example, any list with pleasure and happiness on the list has the commonality that these two goods enjoy, namely experiential quality, and any list with friendship, virtue and self-respect on the list can point to the traits of character and affective states common to these goods. Thus if such a demand is legitimate, there seems nothing intractable about the demand to provide commonalities between the goods postulated by an objective list theory.

Bradley voices another complaint against objective list theories thus:

> [P]luralists must tell us, for example, how to compare the effects on well-being of a certain amount of pleasure with the effect of a certain amount of knowledge...To the extent that the pluralist refuses to tackle these questions she abandons the philosophical project of understanding well-being; she admits defeat. A theory that tells us that A, B, and C are intrinsically good, but does not tell us why those things are on the list or how to weight them, does not give what we initially wanted out of a theory of well-being. We wanted enlightenment, but we are provided instead with a list and told not to look any deeper. This is not theorizing, but a refusal to theorize.

This passage contains at least two separate objections. One is that discussed above (the 'why are *those* things on the list' worry) but there is a distinct worry. This worry is about how much detail the objective list theorist has in their theory. If one were to propose that A, B and C are the only constituents of well-being and then simply *refuse* to tackle the issue of how they are to be weighed against each other then this is certainly a problem. Of course, an objective list theory should either tackle these questions or, at least, tackle the issue of why such questions cannot be answered.

Bradley's objection shows that a very negative and dogmatic kind of objective list theory is unsatisfying for that reason. But this type of objection applies to all theories of well-being. What it highlights is that there is much more work to do than simply specifying what is to go on the list. But equivalent worries apply to hedonism and desire-fulfilment theories.

Take hedonism first. Hedonists need to provide, for example, an account of how to weight: (a) the various elements of a pleasure experience, in calculating the prudential value of a pleasure; (b) the various elements of a pain experience, in calculating the prudential disvalue of a pain; and (c) how to trade off prudential value and disvalue from pleasure and pain in determining someone's overall level of well-being. It is not obvious how to compare (i) a pain/pleasure that is extremely intense but short lasting against (ii) a pain/pleasure that is mild but long-lasting. Nor is it obvious how one arrives at someone's *overall* level of well-being from their level of pleasure and pain. Nor is it obvious that there is one homogeneous kind of e.g. pain (compare, for instance, emotional heartache with the feeling of burning one's hand or with the feeling of having one's finger crushed), and if so one must find a way of comparing different types of pain (or explaining why there is some common, comparable, pain experience that they all have in common).

Moving now to desire-fulfilment theory, we might ask of such a theory how it calculates the prudential value of the fulfilment of a desire and how it weighs desire-fulfilments against non-fulfilments. A very simple form of the theory has an answer, in terms of the intensity of the desire, such that desiring P to degree 10 and it being the case that P has prudential value of + 10 (and desiring P to degree 10 and it being the case that not-P has prudential disvalue of −10). But any more sophisticated desire-fulfilment theory, such as one that takes the relevant desires to be those that meet some counterfactual condition or to be those of a relevant counterpart, will have work to do in specifying exactly how much prudential value or disvalue a desire-fulfilment or non-fulfilment has.

Overall, then, Bradley is right that it is unsatisfying if an objective list theory says *nothing* about e.g. relative weightings. But even if that applies to all extant objective list theories this does not constitute an objection to objective list theories *as such*. It shows that objective list theorists have work to do, and they might have an especially large degree of it, but it is nonetheless work of the same *type* that hedonists and desire-fulfilment theorists must do.

2 Alienation

One common objection to objective list theories is that they are elitist or paternalistic. If this is the claim that the objective list theory says that people should be *compelled* to have the constituents of the list then this objection is mistaken. The objective list theory, like all theories of well-being, is in no way a theory of what people ought to be compelled to have. To see why, note that one could combine the objective list theory with the most stringent anti-paternalism one could imagine. Thus objective list theories have no special connection to paternalism. And the same goes for all other theories of well-being. They do not themselves deliver paternalistic or anti-paternalistic verdicts.

A more sophisticated objection to the objective list theory is that objective list theories are *alienating* or fail to be sufficiently sensitive to the cares and concerns of the agent. An influential way of putting the worry is thus:

> It would be an intolerably alienated conception of someone's good to imagine that it might fail in any way to engage him.[9]

One could develop this idea in a number of ways. One way is the thought that a conception of well-being is problematic if it allows that a person could have a very high level of well-being even if they were affectively unengaged. That is, that their level of well-being was completely unrelated to their pleasures, desires, concerns, volitions, and aims.

This objection is certainly intuitive. It is a *significant* mark against a theory of well-being if it delivers the result that someone has a high level of well-being even though they are utterly miserable and unhappy, or in constant severe pain. And more generally, it seems plausible that a theory of well-being *must* preserve some connection between the things that are good for a person and how they feel and what they care about.

This alienation worry certainly applies to some objective list theories. It clearly applies to *knowledgism*, as described above. It is easy to imagine someone with a lot of knowledge but who was not *interested in* knowledge, did not *want* knowledge, did not *care* about it. Moreover, it is easy to imagine such a person being extremely unhappy.

For these reasons, *knowledgism* leaves open the possibility of someone's having a very high level of well-being despite being completely indifferent to what is purported to be good for them and despite being very miserable. This is clearly a major objection to *knowledgism*. A conception of well-being that said that only knowledge had prudential value is problematic in giving rise to the possibility of such a radical degree of disconnection between what is good for a person (according to the theory) and their affective states.

Does this objection generalise to all objective list theories? At the moment it is hard to say. For whilst knowledgism clearly is an alienating conception of well-being we do not have a clear enough idea of what it takes for a theory of well-being to be alienating. One suggestion is that a theory of well-being is alienating if it is inconsistent with the following thesis:

Attitude-dependence: G is non-instrumentally good for S only if S desires G.

That is, one might think that all and only theories consistent with attitude-dependence are non-alienating.

There are two problems with taking attitude-dependence to be the condition that a theory must meet if it is to avoid alienation. First, the criterion mistakenly classifies as alienating at least some theories that do not seem to be alienating theories of well-being. Second, the criterion begs the question against objective list theories.

On the first problem, one reason to think that whether a theory is alienating is not a matter of whether it is consistent with attitude-dependence is that *hedonism* is inconsistent with attitude-dependence but seems to be a clear case of a non-alienating theory. After all, hedonism says that pleasure is good for you *whether or not you desire it* (and vice versa for pain). Consider this case:

Miserable Maud: Maud is a fully committed ascetic. She thinks that all pleasure is the devil's work and forbidden by her deity. As a result she desires to never feel pleasure and hates the idea of it. Unbeknownst to Maud, she has extremely pleasurable dreams on a nightly basis, dreams that she does not recall upon waking.

Hedonism says that Maud's pleasures are good for her, despite her not desiring them. So hedonism is inconsistent with attitude-dependence. But hedonism does not seem to be an *alienating* theory of well-being.[10]

Similarly, imagine a theory of well-being that said that self-respect and happiness are the only prudential goods (and they are good for someone whether or not that person desires them). Then consider this case:

> **Negative Norman**: Norman is raised by a religious cult that convinces him that he is worthless and that he should not aspire to feel good about himself or his life. As a result he not only lacks self-respect and happiness but ceases even to desire these things.

The self-respect and happiness theory says that self-respect and happiness would be good for Norman, irrespective of his lack of desire for them. The view thus rejects attitude-dependence. But it does not seem to be an alienating conception of well-being. It does not seem problematically alienating for the view that it gives the result that self-respect and happiness would be good for Norman. Thus rejecting attitude-dependence does not seem to be a good test of whether a theory of well-being is alienating.

On the second problem, note that if we were to interpret the idea that a theory of well-being must avoid being alienating as the idea that a theory of well-being must accept attitude-dependence then we beg the question against the objective list theorist. Remember that alienation was supposed to constitute a problem for objective list theories, an independent piece of evidence against such views. Remember too that rejecting attitude-dependence is what *makes* something an objective list theory; all objective list theories violate attitude-dependence simply by being objective list theories.[11] So if the alienation constraint just *is* the denial of the objective list theory's main claim, it cannot be put forward by opponents of objective list theories as an *independent* reason to reject that view.

For these two reasons it would be a mistake to interpret the idea that a theory of well-being must avoid being alienating as the idea that a theory of well-being must accept attitude-dependence. We therefore need some other criterion for determining when a theory of well-being is alienating, some other specification of what the anti-alienation constraint amounts to. (For much more detailed discussion of how exactly to formulate an anti-alienation constraint, see the appendix 'Alienation and attitude-dependence'.)

Remember how wide the class of possible objective list theories is. Whilst some objective list theories – such as *knowledgism* – provide alienating conceptions of well-being, this does not clearly apply to *all* objective list theories. An objective list theorist might argue that their particular theory avoids alienation because of the nature of the goods on their list. Remember our example OLT *three goods*, which claims that pleasure, friendship and achievement are on the list. Each of the three goods is closely connected to the affective, attitudinal or volitional states of the person. For example, a person who experiences pleasure is in the affective states that constitute pleasure, the person who achieves something has a *volition* towards the outcome that they have attained, and a person who has friendship has the attitudes of concern and enjoyment that are constitutive of friendship.[12]

In light of this someone proposing the *three goods* view might claim that their theory (in stark contrast with *knowledgism*) is non-alienating. It rules out the possibility of someone having a high level of well-being whilst being left affectively cold.

Someone might think that the reply in the previous paragraph does not fully address the alienation worry because someone could have these three goods whilst still lacking a *second-order* desire to be in those states.[13] Because *three goods*, like all objective list theories, endorses attitude-independence, it is committed to the claim that the presence or absence of such desires is irrelevant to whether these items contribute to well-being. These three goods are the things that contribute to prudential value, whether you desire them or not.

The objector might argue that for this reason the alienation intuition is thereby left unsatisfied because there is this possibility of an agent who does not care about the things that, according to *three goods*, hold prudential value for them. One might then generalise this to all other OLT theories, given their rejection of attitude-dependence. Yet, as we saw above, whether a theory accepts attitude-dependence does not seem to be a good test of whether a theory is alienating.

To summarise what we have seen so far, it is clear that at least some objective list theories, such as *knowledgism*, are problematically alienating. They provide theories of well-being that allow a person to have a high level of well-being despite being utterly miserable and despite being in no way moved by the things that are good for them (according to the theory).

What remains to be seen is whether this problem afflicts *all* objective list theories. This would be the case if the problem stems simply from rejecting attitude-dependence. If that is so then all objective list theories will be vulnerable to this objection of providing alienating conceptions of well-being.

What is left open here is whether a theory can reject attitude-dependence, as all objective list theories do, whilst still providing a non-alienating conception of well-being.

3.4 Conclusion

In this chapter we have looked at objective list theories. What such theories have in common is that they reject attitude-dependence, they reject the claim that for something to be good for someone they must desire it. We have seen that the class of objective list theories is enormous. There can be monistic forms, which claim that just one thing is desire-independently good for us, or pluralistic forms, which claim that at least two things are desire-independently good for us. We also distinguished brute forms of the view, which claim that there is no explanation of the goods they identify, from forms of OLT which do claim that an explanation can be provided for why the goods on the list have prudential value.

Unlike in the previous chapters it is difficult to supply a definitive summary of the objections and merits of objective list theories because so much depends on the details of the view. Nonetheless, we saw that there are certain kinds of criticisms typically levelled at objective list theories and the various kinds of responses that they might give. One objection, which I return to in an appendix to this chapter, was that objective list theories are alienating.

Another objection was that a theory which provides no explanation of the goods on the list is thereby less theoretically satisfying. For that reason it makes sense for us to now look at perfectionist theories. Such theories are ambitious forms of explanatory objectivism. They reject attitude-dependence, they are typically pluralistic, and they try to supply a comprehensive explanation for all of the goods on the list.

Comprehension questions

1   Why are objective list theories well placed to avoid the scope problem and the experience machine objection?
2   Are any objective list theories vulnerable to the experience machine objection? If so, why? If not, why not?
3   Is hedonism a form of objective list theory? If so, why? If not, why not?
4   Can *three goods* provide a stronger response to the alienation worry than *knowledgism*?

Notes

1   I put this claim simply in terms of 'desires' for simplicity. Sometimes the relevant claim is put in terms of the wider category of 'pro attitudes' (a category that includes desires but also other kinds of positive response, such as liking, preference, etc.). All of the discussion below applies to this wider formulation of the view also.
2   For much more detailed discussion of attitude-dependence and attitude-independence see the appendix to this chapter.
3   For discussion of monism and pluralism in this area see Fletcher (2016), Lin (2015, 2016).
4   Given this characterisation of OLT one can think of hedonism as a monistic objective list theory. For hedonists claim that pleasure is good for you even if you do not desire it. Of course the vast majority of people do desire pleasure but that does not affect hedonism's attitude-independence. If you *didn't* desire pleasure it would still be good for you, if hedonism is true. For further discussion of pleasure and attitude-independence see the appendix to this chapter.
5   This is not strictly the case. One might have an objective list theory about the well-being of agents or people and include within the class of humans or people some non-human animals. But we can leave aside that complication here.
6   See Kitcher (1999).
7   I discuss views of this general type in the chapter on perfectionism.
8   See Bradley (2009: 16).
9   See Railton (2003: 47).
10   You might disagree here, using the case of Miserable Maud to argue that hedonism *is* an alienating conception of well-being.

11 Note, this is not to say that the alienation constraint definitely is not attitude-dependence. Rather, the point is that alienation was supposed to provide an independent reason for rejecting objective list theories. But if the alienation constraint just is the denial of objective list theories then we do not have an independent objection to objective list theories.

12 For discussion of whether an OLT theorist can make this kind of reply see Lin (2015).

13 Indeed, they might in some cases desire *not* to be in those states.

References

Objective list theories in general

Finnis, John (1980). *Natural Law and Natural Rights* (Clarendon Press).

Fletcher, Guy (2016). 'Objective List Theories' in G. Fletcher (ed.), *Routledge Handbook of Philosophy of Well-Being* (Routledge).

Hooker, Brad (2015). 'The Elements of Well-Being'. *Journal of Practical Ethics*, 3(1): 15–35.

Lin, Eden (2015). 'The Subjective List Theory of Well-Being'. *Australasian Journal of Philosophy*, 1–16. http://doi.org/10.1080/00048402.2015.1014926, accessed 22 December 2015.

Moore, Andrew (2000). 'Objective Human Goods' in B. Hooker and R. Crisp (eds.), *Well-Being and Morality: Essays in Honour of James Griffin* (Oxford University Press).

Murphy, Mark (2001). *Natural Law and Practical Rationality* (Cambridge University Press).

Rice, Christopher (2013). 'Defending the Objective List Theory of Well-Being', *Ratio*, 26(2): 196–211.

Objections to objective list theories

Bradley, Ben (2009). *Well-being and Death* (Oxford University Press).

Alienation

Railton, Peter (2003). 'Facts and Values' in Peter Railton, *Facts, Values and Norms* (Cambridge University Press).

Rosati, Connie S. (1996). 'Internalism and the Good for a Person'. *Ethics*, 106(2): 297–326.

Sarch, Alexander (2011). 'Internalism About a Person's Good: Don't Believe It'. *Philosophical Studies*, 154(2): 161–184.

Monism and pluralism

Heathwood, Chris (forthcoming). 'Monism and Pluralism about Value' in Iwao Hirose and Jonas Olson (eds.), *Oxford Handbook of Value Theory* (Oxford University Press).

Lin, Eden (2016). 'Monism and Pluralism' in G. Fletcher (ed.), *Routledge Handbook of Philosophy of Well-Being* (Routledge).

Objective list theories and Explanation

Fletcher, Guy (2013). 'A Fresh Start for the Objective List Theory of Well-Being'. *Utilitas*, 25(2): 206–220.

Hurka, Thomas (1993). *Perfectionism* (Oxford University Press).

Kitcher, Philip (1999). 'Essence and Perfection'. *Ethics*, 110(1): 59–83.

Appendix

Alienation and attitude-dependence

A.1 Introduction

In the previous chapter we saw that a common objection to objective list theories is that they are *alienating*. This is often motivated by appeal to this kind of thought, expressed by Railton:

It would be an intolerably alienated conception of someone's good to imagine that it might fail in any way to engage him.[1]

Many who press this alienation worry against objective list theories think that objective list theories provide alienating conceptions of well-being precisely *because* the theories are committed to this attitude-independence claim:

> **Attitude-independence**: it is *not* the case that G is (non-instrumentally) good for S only if S desires G.[2]

Those who object to objective list theories on the grounds of being alienating typically suggest that the only way to avoid providing an alienating conception of well-being is by rejecting attitude-independence in favour of some form of attitude-dependence such as the following:

> **Attitude-dependence**: G is (non-instrumentally) good for S only if S desires G.

(Henceforth I often omit the 'non-instrumentally', for the sake of readability. All claims about what is good for should be taken to be about what is non-instrumentally good for, unless otherwise specified.)

Thus it is commonly supposed that the distinction between theories according to which well-being is attitude-independent and theories according to which well-being is attitude-dependent also divides theories that are alienating from ones that are not alienating. We can represent this suggestion thus:

Table 3.1

Alienating conceptions of well-being	Non-alienating conceptions of well-being
Attitude-independent theories	Attitude-dependent theories

In this appendix, we will ask whether this is correct. In particular, we will look to see whether a theory of well-being can only avoid being alienating by accepting the attitude-dependence thesis stated above. This is important for two reasons. First, in order to understand the strength of the case against the objective list theorist. Second, because much contemporary work in the philosophy of well-being focuses not on directly arguing for and against particular theories of well-being but, rather, on assessing different attitude-dependence theses.[3]

A.2 Different anti-alienation constraints

Railton's suggestion seems very plausible. It is a major mark against a theory of well-being if it holds that an agent's engagement is completely irrelevant to their well-being. In order to assess this alienation objection to objective list theories it is vital to examine what *exactly* this concern about alienation is supposed to be and how plausible it is. There are *many* different ways of interpreting the idea that a theory of well-being can be, but should not be, alienating. This is, in turn, because there are different ways one could think that well-being is connected to the agent's attitudes. One way of interpreting this concern about alienation is to endorse the attitude-dependence thesis stated above, which we can formulate a little more precisely thus:

> **Attitude-dependence (AD 1)**: G is non-instrumentally good for S at time T1 only if S desires G at T1.[4]

AD1 says that for something to be good for S at a time, S must desire that thing at that time.

One reason to doubt AD1 is that there are cases where something is plausibly good for someone even though they do not *presently* desire that thing. Take this case:

> **Negative Norman**: Norman is raised by a religious cult that convinces him that he is worthless and that he should not aspire to feel good about himself or his life. As a result he not only lacks self-respect and happiness but ceases even to desire these things.

It is plausible that self-respect and happiness would be good for Norman. But AD1 says otherwise; it says that self-respect and happiness are not good for Norman. Why? Because he does not, currently, desire them. But this seems implausible. He'd surely be better off if he had happiness and self-respect even if he does not currently desire them. Cases such as Norman suggest that AD1 ties prudential value too closely to the agent's *current* desires.

If we want a plausible attitude-dependence thesis we thus need to revise AD1. How might we do so? There are various adjustments we might make. One way, familiar from our examination of desire-fulfilment theories,[5] is to move away from the agent's *actual* desires and formulate attitude-dependence in terms of the desires that the agent would have under certain hypothetical circumstances (such as being fully rational, or fully informed or...).[6] Let me postpone that possibility until later (§6).

Another way of revising AD1 is to move away from *desires* for things that the agent presently does *not* have and instead formulate the view in terms of *positive responses* towards things that the agent has *when they have them*. This would be to move to a form of attitude-dependence like this:

> **Attitude-dependence 2 (AD2)**: G is non-instrumentally good for S at T1 only if (i) S responds positively to having G at T1 OR (ii) S would respond positively to G at T1 if S were aware of G at T1.[7]

AD2 differs from AD1 in making the relevant responses those that the agent has towards something *when they have it* rather than beforehand. It also differs in referring to positive responses in general rather than desires in particular.

AD2 gives more plausible results than AD1 when it comes to the case of Norman. He does not desire self-respect or happiness before getting them but it is easy to imagine that upon acquiring them he would then respond positively to them. He would be glad that he has these things, even if he did not desire them in advance. AD2 is thus an improvement over AD1, at least with respect to cases like Norman.

However, there is still a problem that AD2 inherits from AD1. AD2 shares with AD1 a view about the *object* of the attitude that is relevant to prudential value. AD2 holds that for G to be good for someone they must have a positive response *to* G in particular.

One consequence of this is that AD2 generates the result that many pleasures do not have prudential value. That means that AD2 is inconsistent with *hedonism*. Here is why. Suppose hedonism is true, so all and only pleasure has prudential value. Now, take this case:

> **Miserable Maud:** Maud is a fully committed ascetic. She thinks that all pleasure is the devil's work and forbidden by her deity. As a result she desires to never feel pleasure and hates the idea of it. Unbeknownst to Maud, she has extremely pleasurable dreams on a nightly basis, dreams that she does not recall upon waking.

What does hedonism say about this case? It holds that the pleasure Maud experiences during those dreams is good for her. Is this consistent with AD2? No. Maud does not have any positive response towards the pleasures she has when dreaming nor would she respond positively to those pleasures if she was aware of them. She would be horrified! Thus AD2 gives the result that this dream pleasure is not good for Maud. For that reason, AD2 is inconsistent with hedonism.

One might be tempted to downplay the case of *Miserable Maud*, deeming it to be so unusual that we should not afford it much significance in thinking about well-being and alienation. But this problem for AD2 does not only arise only in the unusual case of *Miserable Maud*. AD2 also yields implausible results about the prudential value of pleasure in more mundane cases.

First, take 'flow' experiences, times where you are greatly enjoying and enthralled by some pleasurable activity (pleasure during extreme sports such as surfing or skiing are examples of such pleasures). Though you are experiencing great pleasure your attention is focused actively on the activity or the object of your enjoyment (if your attention was directed anywhere else you would cease to have the flow pleasure). You are 'in the moment' and so do not have any attitudes towards the pleasure that you are experiencing. It seems very plausible that such experiences have prudential value. But, given that, by hypothesis, you lack a positive response towards the pleasure that you are experiencing, AD2 is not satisfied. Thus AD2 must say that such pleasures are not prudentially valuable. But this seems implausible and a point against AD2.

Second, take the example of very young children or babies. Things can be prudentially good and bad for them. It is extremely plausible that, whatever else is non-instrumentally good for babies and young children, pleasure is. However, although young children experience pleasure it is implausible that they have, or could have, positive responses *towards* the pleasure that they experience. However early children develop the capacity to have higher-order attitudes and responses (i.e. attitudes towards attitudes, or responses towards their own responses), it seems plausibly to be after children first experience pleasure. The same might be true for other non-human welfare subjects such as other primates; they experience pleasure but do not have positive responses towards their own attitudes.[8] If we were to accept AD2, we would have to conclude that pleasures are not good for young children and non-human animals (because they do not have the positive responses mentioned in AD2). But that seems mistaken and to cast doubt on AD2.

A defender of AD2 might reply: 'non-human welfare subjects and young children *do* have the higher-order positive responses, or are capable of having them, and so pleasure does in fact respect AD2.'

One reason to doubt that this rescues AD2 is cases of humans with severe mental disabilities. Some kinds of mental disability preclude people from forming higher-order beliefs (beliefs about beliefs). It also seems plausible that at least *some* severe kinds of mental disability could prevent humans who have them from forming second-order positive responses. But it seems implausible that lacking this capacity would mean that any pleasures such humans could experience would not be good for them. In light of this, it appears that AD2 is too restrictive. Whatever connection there is between well-being and attitudes must be different from that suggested by AD2. Can we do any better?

A.3 Object of the positive response

In the previous section we saw that AD2, though more plausible than AD1, struggled with cases where agents do not or cannot form positive responses towards the things that are plausibly good for them.

One amendment we could make to avoid this problem is to drop the restriction on the object of the attitude (what the positive response is a response to) and so move from:

Attitude-dependence 2 (AD2): G is non-instrumentally good for S at T1 only if (i) S responds positively to G at T1 or (ii) S would respond positively to G at T1 if S were aware of G at T1.

TO:

Attitude-dependence 3 (AD3): G is non-instrumentally good for S at T1 only if (i) S responds positively to G at T1 OR G is constituted (at least in part) by S's positive responses.

These two constraints are superficially similar. The main difference is that AD2 requires that for G to be good for S, S must have a positive response *to* G. By contrast, AD3 requires either that S have a positive response to G OR that G itself be something that is (at least in part) one of S's positive responses.

To understand AD3 better we need to think about positive responses. So far we have said little about what positive responses are. Nonetheless it seems plausible that pleasures are, themselves, positive responses.[9] Thus one way of having a positive response is to feel pleasure. If pleasures themselves are positive responses then whenever someone feels pleasure some positive response is *necessarily* present. Importantly, that response may not be towards the pleasure itself, it might be towards any number of other objects (a sensation, a person, etc.). But nonetheless, *whenever* there is pleasure present, there is some positive response present. That is what I mean by saying that pleasure is a positive response.

Going back to our problem cases for AD2, does AD3 do any better? Can AD3 allow that 'flow' cases of pleasure are good for those who experience them, that pleasure is good for infants, that Maud's dreams are good for Maud, and that pleasures are good for welfare subjects unable to form higher-order responses?

The answer in each case is plausibly yes. AD3 is satisfied in each case because the pleasure in each case *is* a positive response. Thus there is a positive response present every time pleasure is present. This enables AD3 to avoid the problem cases for AD2 because it allows pleasures to be good for agents even in the absence of (higher-order) positive responses to those pleasures.

In a *flow* case of pleasure, the presence of the pleasure entails that there is some positive response even though, because the agent is so focused on their activity, the object of that positive response is not the pleasure they are experiencing but something else (perhaps the focus of their attention). Infants who feel pleasure *necessarily* have a positive response because a pleasure is, itself, a positive response. In the case of Miserable Maud, her pleasurable dreams are positive responses. Thus there is a positive response present (even though she certainly would not ever hold a positive response *towards* her own pleasurable dreams). Finally, in the case of welfare subjects that are unable to form higher-order responses – positive responses towards their own positive responses – this is no bar to pleasure being good for them. If they can experience pleasure then any time they do so they experience positive responses, thus satisfying AD3.

In these cases, AD3 yields the result that the pleasures contribute to the person's well-being. Given their respective results in cases such as infants, flow pleasures, Miserable Maud, and cognitively simple welfare subjects, AD3 is superior to AD2.

A.4 Which theories of well-being are compatible with AD3?

I mentioned above that AD2 was incompatible with hedonism. This was because even if pleasures are themselves (at least partly) positive responses, we saw that it is not true in *every* case of prudentially valuable pleasure that the person has a positive response *to that pleasure itself.* By contrast, AD3 is compatible with hedonism. Whenever someone experiences pleasure there is a positive response present (because pleasure is itself a positive response). Thus AD3 is consistent with hedonism. More generally, any theory of well-being will be compatible with AD3 as long as the items that it claims have prudential value are wholly, or partly, comprised of positive responses.

To see how this worry applies beyond pleasure, take friendship as an example of a putative prudential good. Friendship is plausibly at least partly a matter of feeling certain positive responses. It is an essential to friendship that you *care* about your friend. If so, friendship is another putative prudential good that respects AD3. Here is one more example. Self-respect *is* (in part) a positive attitude towards oneself. One cannot have self-respect without this positive response. Thus self-respect is yet another good that is compatible with AD3.

In light of this, it is clear that a wide range of theories are compatible with AD3. Furthermore, there is no bar to an *objective list theory* from being compatible with AD3. For example, take an objective list theory that claims that pleasure, self-respect and friendship are the only prudential goods. Every one of these goods is partly constituted by positive responses and so compatible with AD3. Thus the theory as a whole respects AD3.

What should we conclude from this? It seems that we should hold the following claim: *if* a theory must respect AD3 to avoid being alienating then this anti-alienation constraint does not, itself, rule out hedonism nor does it rule out *all* objective list theories (though it will rule out some).

A.5 Is AD3 enough to avoid alienation?

Many who press the alienation worries against objective list theories will reject the suggestion that compatibility with AD3 suffices for a theory to avoid being an alienating conception of well-being. They might claim that AD3 does not do justice to the anti-alienation constraint on prudential value because it is too permissive. Why is it too permissive? Precisely because it does not require that someone has a positive response *to* G in order for G to be good for them.

What can we do to avoid a stand-off here? How can we make progress? I think that there are two ways we might try to make progress. First, we can look at the role of the attitude-dependence/anti-alienation constraint in the context of the theory of well-being. Second, we can make sure that we have not overlooked a more restrictive form of attitude-dependence – something stronger than AD3 but that can also avoid the problems that afflicted AD2.

Getting anti-alienation constraints to do dialectical work

Turning, first, to the dialectical importance of the anti-alienation constraint, remember that a common argument against objective list theories is that they provide *alienating* conceptions of well-being. We saw in the chapter on objective list theories that what objective list theories have in common is their acceptance of this claim:

> **Attitude-independence**: it is *not* the case that G is non-instrumentally good for S only if S desires G.

The alienation worry is typically pressed against objective list theories because such theories reject the attitude-dependence of prudential value by claiming that something can be good for someone even if they lack a desire for it. Thus it is supposed to be a problem for objective list theories, and evidence against them, that they do not satisfy an alienation constraint on well-being. This dialectical role of the anti-alienation/internalist constraint is helpfully described by Rosati thus:

> Theorists about the good do not always explicitly endorse internalism. But it must lie behind a now standard strategy for defending...subjectivist theories of the good...and so must partly explain the popularity of these views.[10]

Given this background, if we were to construe the worry about alienation in the manner of AD1 (or AD2) we have a constraint too close to the claim that marks the disagreement between objective list theorists and their opponents. Objective list theories violate AD1 because the denial of AD1 *just is* what makes something an objective list theory.

To put it another way, objecting to objective list theories about well-being that they violate AD1 begs the question against the objective list theorist. It does this because AD1 is simply the denial of the objective list theory, rather than an independent claim that can be used to undermine the objective list theory.

It is important to be clear on the point here. The point is *not* that AD1 is *false* because it begs the question against objective list theories. It may well be that AD1 is true (and so objective list theories are false). The point is that if someone were to argue against objective list theories on the grounds that it does not respect a plausible anti-alienation constraint, it would be unsatisfying if the constraint in question just turned out to be simply the negation of what objective list theories hold.

Given the above, we can conclude that *if* the anti-alienation constraint really is best interpreted as AD1 and if this is indeed a real constraint on theories of well-being, then objective list theories are all false. However, if the alienation constraint just *is* the denial of the objective list theory's main tenet, it cannot be put forward by objective list theories opponents as an *independent* reason to reject that view.

In light of this it seems clear that AD1 is too close to the denial of objective list theories' main claim to provide an independent piece of evidence against objective list theories. An important question then is whether AD3 can do any better. Can AD3 perform a useful dialectical function in adjudicating between different theories of well-being?

Here is one reason to think that it can. We noted that *some* objective list theories are compatible with AD3 (and that none are compatible with AD1); it is clear that other objective list theories of well-being will be incompatible with AD3.

Take a theory of well-being that says that what is good for a person is that they make maximal use of their talents and live within and work to preserve certain kinds of social structures. This view is incompatible with AD3. One could easily make use of one's talents and live within and work to preserve certain social structures whilst deriving absolutely no enjoyment or happiness in doing so. One could do this and be lonely, self-loathing, miserable, depressed and so on. What makes this theory of well-being monstrous and alienating is, I take it, that it ignores the agent's affective life completely. It says that simply doing certain kinds of work is good for you *however* that makes you feel.

AD3 offers a reason to reject this kind of theory of well-being, along with any other that allows someone's well-being to be enhanced by things with no connection to their positive responses. AD3 is thus able to show why some theories of well-being are unacceptably alienating. Importantly, it can show why many objective list theories will be alienating without begging the question against all objective list theorists. AD3 thus seems able to play an interesting dialectical role in the debate about well-being and alienation, by giving a plausible reason to rule out certain theories of well-being but without straightforwardly begging the question against all objective list theories.

There are then at least two reasons to prefer AD3 to something stronger, something like AD1 and AD2. AD3 gives plausible answers in cases that make trouble for AD1 and AD2. AD3 also has a claim to capturing the anti-alienation worry without settling the debate between objective list theorists and their opponents (given that one can accept AD3 and be an objective list theorist, or a hedonist, or a perfectionist, or a desire-fulfilment theorist).

A.6 A plausible stronger claim than AD3?

In deciding whether AD3 is the best articulation of the anti-alienation constraint, we should check to make sure that we have not overlooked some alternative. This is because someone might grant that AD3 is *more* plausible than AD1 and AD2 but still claim that a mistake was made in moving from these to AD3.

Earlier I postponed discussion of the idea that one way to improve AD1 is to move away from the agent's actual present desires and instead think about their *idealised* desires of some sort. Let us examine that idea now. Here is AD1:

> **Attitude-dependence 1 (AD 1)**: G is non-instrumentally good (/bad) for S at T1 only if S desires G (/is averse to G) at T1.

In light of its problems, someone might urge that we adopt, in its place:

> **Attitude-dependence 4 (AD 4)**: G is non-instrumentally good (/bad) for S at T1 only if S's idealised counterpart would desire G (/be averse to G) at T1.[11]

There are a number of possible difficulties for AD4. What is important to determine is the extent to which these difficulties are peculiar to AD4's *specific* formulation and how many will afflict any anti-alienation constraint that focuses on desires of idealised counterparts of the agent. Here are some possible difficulties for AD4.

First, until we have a description of the relevant idealising conditions, we cannot really assess AD4. How does S differ from S's idealised counterpart? Do they have more information (if so, how much?)? What kind of information do they have? Are they more rational (if so, to what degree?)?

Second, it needs to be that the desires of the idealised counterparts are plausibly for things that are good for the non-ideal agent. This requires striking a delicate balance. If we idealise too little we may not get the right results (because the agent is too *similar* to the original agent). It seems possible for a *moderately* idealised form of Norman to retain the problematic beliefs that prevent him from desiring happiness or self-respect for himself.

On the other hand, if we idealise too much then we run the risk of getting problematic results because of (a) what it would be like to be such an idealised agent or (b) there being too big a gap between the real agent and their idealised counterpart. Taking (a) first, to borrow a point from the discussion of ideal desire-fulfilment theories, it seems possible that an idealised counterpart of S might desire the destruction of all humanity (perhaps because they know all of the terrible things that humans do). But it would be very problematic if this meant that death was good for S. So the ideal conditions must be ones that do not introduce problematic consequences of this sort.

Moving now to the other problem (i.e. (b)), a problem with idealising S a lot and taking their desires to act as a constraint on what is good for S is to open up a gap for an alienating conception of well-being. This is because if idealised S's desires are too dissimilar from S's desires, because of features of being idealised, then we have an anti-alienation constraint that is insufficiently sensitive to the *actual* agent's desires, etc. After all, if the idealised agent would desire [a, b and c], but the actual agent desires [g, h, i] it seems like a clear case of an alienating conception of well-being to hold that only [g, h, i] are good for the agent, because only these are desired by their counterpart.

I mentioned above that some difficulties with AD4 will stem from particular features of AD4. Someone who defends an anti-alienation constraint that focuses on idealised desires will have to either reject the problems just outlined or provide some reason to think that they only apply to AD4 but would not apply to some better-formulated constraint. Perhaps that can be done but note the range of cases that such a constraint would have to get right:

1   cases of people whose psychology or upbringing prevents them from desiring even their own self-respect and happiness
2   flow pleasures
3   pleasures in infants
4   pleasures experienced in dreaming
5   pleasures experienced by humans who have reduced mental capacities
6   pleasures experienced by non-human welfare subjects.

Whether there is a form of idealised desires anti-alienation constraint that can get all of these cases right is an interesting question, one that we cannot hope to settle here.

A.7 Conclusion

In this appendix we examined the purported anti-alienation constraint on theories of well-being. The aim was to understand what the most plausible form of this constraint might be and, subsequently, to see whether it undermines all objective list theories of well-being.

We have seen that some ways of interpreting this constraint (AD1 and AD2) are implausible because they rule out some clear candidates for prudential value. We then examined a weaker constraint, AD3. This constraint avoided the problems of AD1 and AD2 whilst providing a plausible interpretation of the worry about alienation (as evidenced by its ruling out some clearly alienating conceptions of well-being). We examined whether AD3 was sufficient or whether the anti-alienation constraint is actually a stronger constraint, one based on the desires of an idealised counterpart of the agent.

The main conclusions of this appendix were:

1   *If* AD1 or AD2 is a genuine constraint on theories of well-being then all objective list theories are false.
2   *If* AD3 is a real constraint on theories of well-being then only some objective list theories are ruled out by it.
3   It is unclear whether we should adopt AD3 or some stronger constraint (AD4), one focused on the idealised desires of the agent.

Comprehension questions

1   Suppose that pleasure is at least partly constituted by positive responses. Would that mean that a creature unable to form second-order responses cannot feel pleasure?
2   Would every idealised counterpart of Norman desire that Norman be happy?
3   What is the difference between AD2 and AD3?

Further question

1   Could we stick with AD3 or does avoiding alienating conceptions of well-being require something more like AD4?

Notes

1   See Railton (2003).
2   I put this claim simply in terms of 'desires' for simplicity. Sometimes the relevant claim is put in terms of the wider category of 'pro attitudes' (a category that includes desires but also other kinds of positive response, such as liking, preference, etc.). All of the discussion below applies to this wider formulation of the view also.
3   For further discussion see Rosati (1996), Sarch (2011), Hawkins (2014), Hall and Tiberius (2016).
4   AD1 is almost identical to attitude-dependence – it is just slightly more specific. Note that AD1 proposes only a *necessary* condition of something being good for someone, not a sufficient condition.
5   See chapter 2.
6   See chapter 2.
7   This constraint is almost identical to one proposed by Hawkins (2014).
8   This kind of case might also be reason to doubt theories of the nature of pleasure that identify pleasure with attitudes towards (e.g.) sensations. Many thanks to Chris Woodard for discussion here.
9   Such a move is explicitly endorsed by Hawkins (a proponent of AD2): 'I intend the idea of positive response/positive registration to be as broad as possible, to include both positive *feelings* and positive *thoughts*…I do, however, intend positive response to be *mental*. Minimally, for something to register positively with A, it must enter A's conscious awareness in a way that is positively valenced.' See Hawkins (2014: 527).
10 See Rosati (1996: 299).
11 This will be reminiscent of the idealised forms of desire-fulfilment theory we came across in chapter 2.

Further reading

Fletcher, Guy (2013). 'A Fresh Start for the Objective List Theory of Well-Being'. *Utilitas*, 25(2): 206–220.

Fletcher, Guy (2016). 'Objective List Theories' in G. Fletcher (ed.), *Routledge Handbook of Philosophy of Well-Being* (Routledge).

Hall, Alicia and Valerie Tiberius (2016). 'Well-Being and Subject Dependence' in G. Fletcher (ed.), *Routledge Handbook of Philosophy of Well-Being* (Routledge).

Hawkins, Jennifer (2014). 'Well-Being, Time and Dementia'. *Ethics*, 124(3): 507–542.

Railton, Peter (2003). 'Facts and Values' in Peter Railton, *Facts, Values and Norms* (Cambridge).

Rosati, Connie S. (1996). 'Internalism and the Good for a Person'. *Ethics*, 106(2): 297–326.

Sarch, Alexander (2011). 'Internalism About a Person's Good: Don't Believe It'. *Philosophical Studies*, 154(2): 161–184.

4 Perfectionist theories of well-being

4.1 Introduction

In the previous chapters we examined hedonism, desire-fulfilment theories, and objective list theories. One of the main challenges to objective list theories was the desirability of giving a rationale for the goods on the list. Put another way, they are under pressure to supply an explanation of *why* X, Y, Z have prudential value. In light of this it makes sense now to examine *perfectionist* theories. Such theories are typically (though not exclusively) pluralistic and supply a rationale for the plurality of goods they identify.

One note of caution before we start: *many* different theories are labelled 'perfectionist' or 'perfectionism'.[1] Some of these theories address different issues from those that concern us here (namely well-being). For example, at least one 'perfectionist' theory is a theory of *morality*, of what we morally ought to do. We must therefore be careful to restrict our interest to perfectionist theories of prudential value, of what contributes and detracts from well-being, in particular.

4.2 Perfectionism formulated

An initial motivation

Some things are good for us. Some (usually different) things are good for car engines, watches, pianos and houses. Deep water is bad for car engines. Sand is bad for watches. Woodworm is bad for pianos. Damp is bad for houses.

A perfectionist about prudential value might urge that this observation should prompt us to look for a common, abstract, recipe that determines when something is good for some entity (be it a person or an artefact). That general recipe, they might urge, is that whether something is good for something depends on the thing in question. Whether something is good for a living creature depends on its nature and the kinds of capacities central to its nature. Let us give a bit more detail to the general outline of a perfectionist story, abstracting from details of particular perfectionist theories as much as possible for the moment.

Let us follow Dorsey in distinguishing three separate elements of a complete perfectionist theory of prudential value thus:[2]

1   General Perfectionism: The good life for an x is determined by what it means to be an x.
2   Identification of the Core Capacities: what it is to be an x involves a specific set of capacities {a, b, c}.
3   Fulfilment of the Core Capacities: A life lived according to capacities {a, b, c} involves certain specific activities {q, r, s}.

This gives us an initial grasp of what a perfectionist theory of well-being is going to be like. But we still need to develop the theory further.

Perfectionism about human well-being

Here is an initial formulation of perfectionism about human well-being:

> **Perfectionism about human well-being:** The good life for a human is deter-mined by human nature. Human nature involves a specific set of capacities. The exercise and development of these capacities is good for humans.

This is highly abstract. There are many places where the theory needs further development and many potential places for disagreement even amongst those who accept that the good life for a human is determined by human nature. In particular there are these two related questions to which different perfectionists can give different answers:

1   Which *capacities* are constitutive of human nature?
2   Which *activities* exercise and develop those capacities?

Here are two possible perfectionist theories, stemming from different answers to these questions:

> **Perfectionism A**: The good life for a human is determined by human nature. Theoretical rationality is constitutive of human nature. Intellectual contemplation exercises and develops this capacity.

> **Perfectionism B:** The good life for a human is determined by human nature. Practical rationality is constitutive of human nature. Political life exercises and develops this capacity.

The difference between Perfectionism A and Perfectionism B is stark (making clear just how much a perfectionist needs to do to move from the abstract characterisation of perfectionism to a full theory). The first form of perfectionism recommends a life of pure intellectual contemplation. The second form of perfectionism recommends a life in politics. Rather than examining further the choice between Perfectionism A and Perfectionism B I will spend the rest of this chapter examining the prospects for perfectionism in general. Thus my focus will be on:

> **(Human) perfectionism:** What is non-instrumentally good for a human is determined by human nature. Human nature involves a specific set of capacities. The exercise and development of these capacities is non-instrumentally good for humans.[3]

(Henceforth I often omit the 'non-instrumentally', for the sake of readability. All claims about what is good for should be taken to be about what is non-instrumentally good for, unless otherwise specified. I also use just 'perfectionism' to refer to this view, for the sake of brevity.)

4.3 Arguments for perfectionism

What arguments can perfectionists give for the view? One strategy that they might employ is a kind of paradigm case argument. They might do so as follows: when we reflect on paradigmatic cases of lives that have very high levels of well-being we find that these lives clearly involve the exercise and development of human capacities. This seems right. It seems very difficult to imagine a life with a high degree of well-being but where the person exercises few, or none, of their human capacities. That is one piece of evidence for perfectionism.

Another argument that the perfectionist can give for their account of well-being is its *flexibility*. Because perfectionism about human well-being is a specific instance of general perfectionism this enables us to derive theories of well-being for non-human animals and other things which have levels of well-being. For example:

> **Gorilla well-being perfectionism**: What is non-instrumentally good for a gorilla is determined by gorilla nature. Gorilla nature involves a specific set of capacities. The exercise and development of these capacities is good for gorillas.

And drawing upon the previous argument for perfectionism – the paradigm case argument – the perfectionist can plausibly say that we find a general trend among paradigmatic cases of high well-being *across* human and non-human animals. The life of a flourishing gorilla seems to be clearly connected to the life in which it exercises and develops the capacities constitutive of its nature. Thus perfectionism fits into a general kind of perfectionism that has flexibility and that gets plausible results about paradigm cases of lives high in well-being of both human and non-human animals.

A third kind of argument that the perfectionist might point to is that perfectionism would nicely cohere with and explain our tendency to think of good lives as 'fully human' and bad lives as somehow 'inhuman' or 'not fully human' along with our tendency to think that whether something is good for a creature depends on whether it fits with, or suits, its *nature*. Though an opponent might note this sort of talk is a little vague, the perfectionist is surely right that we do talk in these ways and that this provides some evidence for the claim that the exercise and development of the capacities constitutive of human nature is good for humans.

In considering these arguments for perfectionism, it is important to remember that the perfectionist does not seek merely to establish a *correlation* between lives high in well-being and lives that involve the exercise and development of human capacities. The holder of perfectionism claims that there is this correlation *because* the exercise and development of human capacities is what is good for us and that this *explains* a person's level of well-being.

To more fully assess perfectionism's strong and weak points we need to know a little more. In particular, we need to know what human nature is, in order to know what exactly perfectionism claims is good and bad for humans. So let us turn to perfectionism's task of establishing a theory of human nature to fit into perfectionism.

4.4 Supplying an account of human nature (I)

Remember that *this* is the perfectionist theory to be examined in the rest of the chapter:

> **Perfectionism:** What is non-instrumentally good for a human is determined by human nature. Human nature involves a specific set of capacities. The exercise and development of these capacities is good for humans.

A task for anyone attracted to perfectionism is to provide an account of human nature. This is quite a task. What constitutes human nature? How might we decide what does? One proposal that might come to mind is to look for what is *unique* to humans and so endorse the following view of human nature:

> **Uniqueness criterion of human nature:** Capacity X is (part of) human nature if and only if X is unique to humans (i.e. no non-human has X).

This criterion has a certain amount of initial plausibility. It amounts to the thought that human nature is tied to what *distinguishes* humans from other things. Unfortunately, it looks vulnerable to a number of different objections.

Objections to the uniqueness criterion

A first problem with the uniqueness criterion is that it leaves open the possibility that there is *no* human nature. This would be the case if there is no capacity X unique to humans. This seems quite problematic in and of itself but things get much worse if we combine the uniqueness criterion with perfectionism. This combination would entail that, if there is no unique human capacity, then *nothing* is good or bad for humans. But that seems extremely implausible! It seems very odd to think that whether something is good or bad for humans depends on whether there is a capacity that is unique to humans, such that if there is no such capacity then *nothing* is good for humans.

A defender of the uniqueness criterion might reply along two lines. First, they might claim that it is implausible that there is no capacity unique to humans. Second, they might claim that the mere possibility of there being no unique capacity in humans is insufficient to reject the criterion.

Against the first reply, it is rather unclear how plausible it is to think that there is no capacity unique to humans. Take *rationality*, a canonical example of the kind of capacity that is (i) sometimes suggested to be unique to humans and (ii) typically suggested by perfectionist theories as a capacity central to prudential value. Is it so difficult to imagine discovering that *some* non-human animal had rationality? Various kinds of evidence suggest that at least some higher primates are rational to at least some extent.[4] But suppose that is not so. Still, even if there is no plausible contender on earth, should we really be confident that there is no other creature with rationality *in the entire universe*?

Luckily, I think that we do not really need to settle this issue. Take the second reply offered by the defender of the uniqueness criterion – the mere possibility of there being no unique capacity in humans is insufficient to reject the criterion. This does not seem right. If it is *possible* that there is no unique human capacity this means that, if perfectionism is true, then it is *possible* that nothing is good or bad for humans. But it does not seem possible that nothing is good or bad for humans. If this is right we must reject one of

i   The possibility that there is no unique human capacity.
ii Perfectionism about human well-being.
iii The uniqueness account of human nature.

Given the plausibility of (i), it looks like we must reject at least one of (ii) and (iii). Given our interest in assessing (ii) we should reject (iii) and look for an alternative.

So far, we have explored problems for the uniqueness criterion that stem from the possibility of there being no capacity unique to humans (so the uniqueness criterion is unsatisfied). Two different objections arise on the assumption that the criterion is satisfied. These are, first, that the criterion can be satisfied by the wrong things and, second, that the satisfaction of the criterion does not have the direct relevance to prudential value that perfectionism needs human nature to have.

The first objection is that if we combine perfectionism with the uniqueness criterion then we must accept that well-being could turn out to be determined by *very* different kinds of capacities from the ones typically offered by perfectionists. For example, suppose it turns out that the only uniquely human capacity is the capacity for throat singing. This, combined with the uniqueness criterion and perfectionism, would deliver the result that the exercise and development of the capacity to throat sing is the *only* thing that has prudential value for humans. But that is implausible.

Defenders of perfectionism and the uniqueness criterion could respond, understandably, by arguing that their *opponent* bears the burden of proof. That is to say, they could respond by saying that the *possibility* of getting unintuitive verdicts is not, itself, an objection unless we have good reason to think that (e.g.) throat singing really is the uniquely human capacity.

That reply seems partially right. Certainly, there is the possibility that the actual uniquely human capacity is something more plausibly connected to human well-being than throat singing is. But notice that perfectionism and the uniqueness criterion are committed to this conditional claim 'If throat singing is the only uniquely human capacity then exercising and developing one's capacity for throat singing is the only thing with prudential value'. And one might think that it is problematic enough for a view if it even generates this conditional conclusion.

The previous objection, that the perfectionism plus uniqueness criterion is committed to implausible conditional conclusions brings out a more general objection to grounding human nature, and thereby well-being, in uniqueness. This objection is that a change in our beliefs about the capacities unique to humans does not look like something that would plausibly *change* our beliefs about prudential value. To take one example, it is clearly the case that non-human animals feel pain and pleasure. Given this, it looks like *if* the uniqueness criterion is true then, upon coming to realise that the capacities for pleasure and pain are not unique to humans, we should feel some rational pressure to give up those beliefs. But this seems implausible. Our judgement that (e.g.) pain is bad for humans would be, and should be, completely unaffected by the discovery that pain is not a unique human capacity. We would not abandon this judgement about the prudential disvalue of pain merely in light of finding that the capacity for pain is not unique to humans.[5]

Conversely, on the positive side of well-being, it looks like, *if* the uniqueness criterion is true, then discovering that (e.g.) throat singing is unique to humans (and that pleasure is not unique to them) should generate some rational pressure to abandon the view that pleasure is non-instrumentally good for humans and to adopt the view that throat singing is the only non-instrumental good for humans. But, I take it, we do not feel any disposition to modify our views along these lines.

What this seems to suggest is that the fact that something is unique to humans itself has no fundamental significance for prudential value. If that is right then perfectionists should reject the *uniqueness* criterion.

4.5 Supplying an account of human nature (II)

If human nature is not simply a matter of what is unique to humans, what else might it be? What if the perfectionist adopts the following proposal:

> **Essence criterion of human nature**: Capacity X is (part of) human nature if and only if X is essential to humans (i.e. no human can lack X).[6]

This criterion has a certain amount of initial plausibility. It amounts to the thought that human nature is tied to what *unifies* humans, what they all have in common. Unfortunately, the criterion seems to be both too inclusive and too restrictive for the perfectionist's purposes.

On the too inclusive side, it looks like lots of well-being-irrelevant capacities are essential to humans. For example, all humans have the capacity to act as a paperweight or to be fired out of a cannon. But the exercise and development of these capacities does not plausibly have prudential value.

On the too restrictive side, it looks like a number of well-being-relevant capacities are not essential to humans. For example, not all humans have the capacity to feel physical pain or pleasure. Given this, the essence criterion seems to rule out physical pleasure and pain from having prudential value and disvalue. But that seems very implausible.

Given the failure of the two proposals for what human nature is, it might be useful to now look at a different way of giving an account of human nature. One feature common to each of the two failed criteria that we have considered so far is that they are *value-neutral*. That is, they aim to identify human nature in a non-evaluative way, as simply the properties *essential* to humans or *unique* to humans. One consequence of that is that the implications of the criteria often wildly diverge from our judgements about *which* capacities and properties are relevant to well-being.

At this point, one might suggest that the defender of perfectionism proceed in a different way. Rather than looking for a purely value-neutral conception of human nature and thinking that well-being is determined by that, one could instead use our judgements about well-being to inform our theory of human nature. So, for example, in looking for a theory of human nature we might be guided by our judgement that physical pleasure and pain are good and bad for humans, rather than (trying to) suspend judgement on what is good and bad for humans whilst investigating human nature. Let us call this way of arriving at an account of human nature the *reflective equilibrium method*. (Notice that it is not a particular account of what human nature is, rather it is a methodological proposal, a proposal for *how* to determine what human nature is.)

Let us look at this reflective equilibrium method for determining what human nature is and see how well it fits with perfectionism. Taking account of the above, someone pursuing this strategy might say that the following are not part of human nature: the capacity to be a paperweight, the capacity to be fired out of a cannon. Furthermore, they might say that it is a constraint on a theory of human nature that it cohere with the claim that physical pain is bad for us and that (at least some) physical pleasure is good for us and that the exercise and development of rationality is good for us. So the following capacities are ruled in and out of our conception of human nature:

Ruled out: the capacity to be a paperweight, the capacity to be fired out of a cannon.

Ruled in: the capacity for rationality, (at least some) physical pleasure, pain.

This is, of course, just the beginning. On this reflective equilibrium method we need to do a lot of work in refining our account of human nature in the light of science and our best judgements about prudential value.

A problem is lurking though. To see that problem, remember the general dialectic. Perfectionism about human well-being is the following view:

Perfectionism: What is non-instrumentally good and bad for a human is determined by human nature. Human nature involves a specific set of capacities. The exercise and development of these capacities is good for humans.

In trying to assess this view we then turned to the question of what human nature is. Having seen two initial proposals fail we then turned to the *reflective equilibrium* method, one where the correct account of human nature can be partly determined by facts about what is good or bad for us.

Here is the problem. If we allow facts about prudential value to determine our account of human nature then, rather than supporting human well-being perfectionism, this actually undermines the perfectionist view. It undermines the view by introducing a problematic kind of circularity where both of the following are true:

human nature DETERMINES facts about well-being
facts about well-being DETERMINE human nature

Where the perfectionist asserts that human well-being is determined by human nature, this *reflective equilibrium* way of developing a theory of human nature suggests that human nature is itself, at least partly, determined by facts about well-being. This proposal therefore threatens to make human nature redundant in the context of perfectionism. It threatens to make it redundant because facts about well-being are themselves serving to determine what human nature is. So human nature itself is determined by facts about well-being, rather than the determinant of them.[7]

Notice that this objection is not, specifically, an objection to developing theories of human nature along the lines of the reflective equilibrium method. Rather, the objection is that developing a theory of human nature in this way *fits badly with perfectionism* by undermining the perfectionist's claim that human nature determines what holds prudential value by allowing human nature to itself be determined by prudential value.

In light of this, it seems that those tempted by perfectionism should eschew a reflective equilibrium method for determining human nature. To adopt this model is to rob perfectionism of its explanatory potential. If this is right then perfectionism needs an account of human nature that is more like – but superior to – the uniqueness and essence accounts we considered earlier.

Hurka's restricted essence proposal

Let us consider one more proposal for the correct account of human nature by taking the essence proposal discussed above but modifying it in a way suggested by Tom Hurka (1993: 16–17):

> **Hurka's criterion of human nature**: Capacity X is (part of) human nature if and only if X is essential to humans (i.e. no human can lack X) 'conditioned on their being living things'.

Though this makes reference to the properties essential to humans this proposal is significantly different from the straightforward essence criterion rejected above. The major difference is that Hurka's criterion focuses on the properties all humans have *as living things*. As Hurka puts it: 'These are essential properties that humans could not have if they were not living; they presuppose life, or are necessarily distinctive of living things.'[8]

Hurka's criterion is more restrictive than the essence criterion rejected above. One of the problems for the essence criterion was that it suggested that the exercise and development of the capacity to be a paperweight, or to be fired out of a cannon, was good for a person (after all these capacities are necessarily had by *all* humans). Hurka's criterion avoids this result. For whilst humans necessarily have the capacity to be a paperweight they only have this *as physical objects*. They do not have this *as living things*. After all, a dead human has the capacity to be a paperweight just as much as a living one. As this makes clear, to understand Hurka's proposal properly we need to take the set of properties that humans necessarily have:

> **Necessary properties of humans**: a, b, c, d, e, f, g, h, i

and then restrict this further by removing any that humans would retain if dead. This gives us the more restricted set:

Necessary properties of living humans: a, b, c, d

Hurka's proposal is that human nature is the latter set, the set of properties that humans necessarily have *if alive*.

Hurka's proposal avoids the problems that are faced by each of the uniqueness proposal and the essence proposal. It is also value neutral so does not threaten to make human nature explanatorily redundant if combined with perfectionism about well-being. For the rest of the chapter I will assume that Hurka's account of human nature is the best for the perfectionist theory of well-being. This is in order to make the theory specific enough to assess. However, my discussion would also be applicable to perfectionist theories that incorporate many other theories of human nature.

4.6 Objections

In this section I will consider some of the main objections to perfectionism. Incorporating Hurka's account of human nature above, the view we are considering is the following:

> **Perfectionism***: What is good for a human is determined by human nature. The exercise and development of the capacities essential to humans conditioned on their being living things is good for humans.

Objection one: the bad side?

The first objection is that perfectionism*, as stated, does not give us a clear idea of how prudential *badness* is determined, or how something gets to be *bad* for someone. Thus this objection is a call for clarification or development of the theory so that it has an account of the things that are bad for us.

There seem to be two possible ways to adapt perfectionism so as to get a theory of what is bad for us:

Non-development of capacities

The non-exercise and non-development of the capacities essential to humans conditioned on their being living things is bad for humans.

Diminishment/loss of capacities

The diminishment of the capacities essential to humans conditioned on their being living things is bad for humans.

Of these two possible ways of adapting perfectionism to get a theory of what is bad for us, which is the most plausible? It seems more plausible that the second thesis – *diminishment* – is the more plausible. For whilst the non-development of essential human capacities might be something that fails to be good for us that does not mean that it is *bad* for us. If we want to preserve a clear distinction between the absence of what is good for us and the presence of what is bad for us then it looks like we need the second perfectionist thesis of what is bad for us. Henceforth I will assume that that is the perfectionist account of what is bad for us, so the full theory is now:

> **Perfectionism****: What is non-instrumentally good or bad for a human is determined by human nature. The exercise and development of the capacities essential to humans conditioned on their being living things is good for humans. The diminishment of the capacities essential to humans conditioned on their being living things is bad for humans.

Objection two: problems with pleasure and pain

It seems undeniable that at least some kinds of pleasure and pain are, respectively, good and bad for us. Take a case of a person enjoying a plea-surable massage and cocktails during a luxury holiday in a beautiful place. By contrast, take some paradigmatic case of something that is bad for someone: a case of mistaken identity that leads to their being captured and painfully tortured for an hour.

It seems highly plausible that a theory of well-being *must* deliver the result that the relaxing holiday massage is good for the person and that the painful torture is bad for the person. The trouble for perfectionism is that it is not clear that it gets the right result in these cases. Why so?

First, as was mentioned above, not all humans have the capacity to experience physical pleasure and pain. Thus it is not true that necessarily all humans, as living things, have the capacity to feel physical pleasure and pain. If that is right, then these capacities cannot be prudential-value determining. After all, perfectionism says that what is good for us is the exercise and development of the capacities constitutive of human nature. But, applying perfectionism**'s account of human nature, the capacities to experience physical pleasure and pain are not constitutive of human nature.

This first problem stemmed from the observation that perfectionism (com-bined with Hurka's account of human nature) does not class physical pleasure and pain within the set of capacities relevant to prudential value and disvalue, given their non-universality. But suppose that this was not true. Suppose that the capacity to experience physical pleasure and pain really is essential to humans conditioned on their being living things. One might *then* be tempted to argue that perfectionism actually can deliver the result that physical pleasure is good for us. Imagine them arguing as follows: 'Perfectionism claims that the exercise and development of the capacities essential to humans conditioned on their being living things is good for humans. The holiday massage involves the exercise of the capacity for physical pleasure. As long as this is one of the human nature-constituting capacities then perfectionism can deliver the result that pleasurable episodes like the massage are good for us. They are good for us because they involve the exercise of the capacity to feel physical pleasure.'

This response has some plausibility. One might worry that feeling physical pleasure, especially sensory pleasures like those from a massage, is too *passive* to count as exercising a capacity.[9] But however problematic that is, there is a much bigger problem with this response. The same reasoning delivers the conclusion that the hour-long torture is also good for us! After all, in an episode of painful torture, we exercise the capacity to feel physical pain in just the same way as, in an episode of pleasurable massage, we exercise the capacity to feel physical pleasure. So if exercising a capacity is what makes something good for us then the torture and the massage are *both* good for us. Thus if a perfectionist claims that the prudential value of physical pleasure stems from its being the exercise of a capacity for physical pleasure they will be unable to block the conclusion that there is also similar prudential value to episodes of physical pain. Each involves the exercise of a capacity to just the same extent.

The perfectionist needs to vindicate the conclusion that torture is bad for us. One move that they might make in support of this is that even if feeling physical pain involves the exercise of our capacity to feel pain, torture also involves the *diminishment* of human capacities.[10] Thus perfectionism can rely on the account of prudential disvalue that we developed earlier – one in terms of the diminishment of the capacities essential to humans – to generate the result that painful torture is bad for us.

It is certainly plausible that some forms of torture diminish (and perhaps destroy) human capacities. The problem for this response, though, is that this is not plausible for *all* of the kinds of physical pain that we think are bad for us. After all, it seems implausible that every pain that is bad for us is one that *necessarily* diminishes human capacities.

Furthermore, thinking that the diminishment of a capacity is always bad for us seems rather implausible as shown by the following case. Suppose you have a dental operation and a moderately effective dose of anaesthetic is given. You feel moderate but bearable pain. In this case we have (1) the giving of the anaesthetic and (2) the pain felt. Which is bad for you and which is good for you? It is obvious that the anaesthetic was good for you and the pain was bad for you. However, the *anaesthetic* clearly diminished your capacity to feel pain (albeit only temporarily) whilst it is far from clear that the moderate pain diminished any of your capacities. If that is right then the perfectionist seems forced to conclude in this case that the pain was not bad for you (it was *good* for you because it exercised your capacity to feel pain) but that the anaesthetic was *bad* for you (because it diminished your capacity to feel pain).

Let us take stock. I have argued that there are a cluster of problems for perfectionism** connected to pleasure and pain. We can summarise these problems as follows:

1   It is unclear that perfectionism** entails that physical pleasure and pain are good for us. This is because the capacity for physical pleasure and pain is not essential to humans (even conditioned on their being living things). So physical pleasure and pain look like well-being-irrelevant capacities, according to perfectionism**.
2   Even if physical pleasure and pain are well-being relevant capacities, physical pleasure and pain *both* involve the exercise of a capacity. So perfectionism** seems to mistakenly classify both as good for us.
3   Things that diminish our capacity to feel physical pain seem to be mistakenly classified as bad for us, by perfectionism**.

Objection three: too restrictive, leaving out rationality

A further objection to perfectionism** is that it faces a dilemma in either having to adopt a controversial view about humans or in being too restrictive with respect to capacities which perfectionists typically want to treat as being relevant to prudential value in humans. Here is how the dilemma arises.

There are cases of severely mentally disabled humans who plausibly lack conscious awareness and rationality. These humans are nonetheless alive. These cases show that rationality (and conscious awareness) are not essential to humans, conditioned on their being alive. Thus, according to perfectionism**, capacities such as rationality are not ones whose exercise and development has prudential value for humans. But this is completely at odds with what most perfectionists think. They almost universally hold that rationality is the main capacity whose exercise and development is good for humans.

If perfectionists want to hold that rationality is a capacity whose exercise and development is good for humans then they must therefore do one of two things. They must either argue that what we typically think of as severely mentally disabled, non-rational, *humans* are not in fact humans, in virtue of lacking rationality.[11] Alternatively, and more plausibly, they need a different account of human nature, one that recognises that rationality is not universal to living humans. But if they make that concession, and allow that humans are not necessarily rational, it is unclear whether perfectionists can consistently hold both (i) that human essence determines prudential value and (ii) that the exercise and development of rationality is good for humans. Holding the second of these claims suggests that at least one aspect of prudential value is not explained by the essence of humans.

4.7 Conclusion

In this chapter we have examined perfectionism about prudential value. We examined the prospects of perfectionism by looking at the various views of human nature it could be combined with and the prospects of each.

A recurring theme is that if perfectionism is to be a genuinely explanatory theory of well-being it faces a very difficult balancing act. It must supply an account of human nature that is independently plausible and well-motivated and that can deliver plausible verdicts about prudential value. This task is made difficult by the fact that many capacities whose exercise seems closely connected to well-being are neither universal in, nor essential to, humans.

A common response at this point is that whilst perfectionism is absolutely correct to note a general correlation between (a) lives that are high in well-being and (b) lives that involve the extensive exercise and development of human capacities, the difficulties identified above mean that we should not conclude from this correlation that there is an explanatory connection between human nature and prudential value. Rather, the correlation is to be explained by the fact that lives that involve the extensive exercise and development of human capacities typically *also* thereby have the features that generate well-being, whatever these might be.[12]

Comprehension questions

1   Why would it be problematic for a perfectionist to treat human nature as the capacity, or set of capacities, *unique* to humans?
2   Why would it be problematic for a perfectionist to identify human nature with the set of capacities that it is good for us to exercise and develop?
3   Why might perfectionism struggle to accommodate the claim that pain is bad for us?

Notes

1 Bradford (2016).
2 Dorsey (2010). I make some slight alterations to Dorsey's presentation.
3 I make some slight alterations to the above formulation in order to make clearer how it contrasts with the other theories examined in this book.
4 See Andrews (2014) and references.
5 To put the point another way, were you at all tempted to give up the view that pain is bad for you when you discovered that non-humans feel pain?
6 Here I am assuming, on behalf of this proposal, that the necessary properties of something are identical to its essence. A perfectionist might want to resist that. The question is how to do so. In the next subsection I consider such a proposal.
7 For discussion of this problem for perfectionism – in the context of Richard Kraut's (2007) developmentalism – see Sobel (2010). Perfectionists will have replies to this objection. One possible reply is that the objection equivocates on 'determines'.
8 Hurka (1993: 16).
9 Bradford (2016).

10 For discussion of this see Kraut (2007: 150), Fletcher (2009), Sobel (2010).
11 For discussion of these issues see Kitcher (1999), Williams (1985: chapter 3).
12 See the third factor objection in chapters 1 and 2.

References

Andrews, Kristin (2014). 'Animal Cognition'. *The Stanford Encyclopedia of Philosophy* (Fall Edition), Edward N. Zalta (ed.).http://plato.stanford.edu/archives/fall2014/entries/cognition-animal, accessed 22 December 2015.

Bradford, Guy (2016). 'Perfectionism' in G. Fletcher (ed.), *Routledge Handbook of Philosophy of Well-Being* (Routledge).

Dorsey, Dale (2010). 'Three Arguments for Perfectionism', *Noûs*, 44(1): 59–79.

Fletcher, Guy (2009). 'Review of Richard Kraut's, What is Good And Why: The Ethics of Well-Being'. *Analysis Reviews*, 69(3): 576–578.

Hurka, Thomas (1993). *Perfectionism* (Oxford University Press).

Kitcher, Philip (1999). 'Essence and Perfection'. *Ethics*, 110(1): 59–83.

Kraut, Richard (2007) *What is Good and Why: The Ethics of Well-Being* (Harvard University Press).

Sobel, David (2010). 'The Limits of the Explanatory Power of Developmentalism'. *Journal of Moral Philosophy*, 7(4): 517–527.

Williams, Bernard Arthur Owen (1985). *Ethics and the Limits of Philosophy* (Harvard University Press).

Further reading

Aristotle. *Nicomachean Ethics.*

Brink, David (2003). *Perfectionism and the Common Good* (Oxford University Press).

Mason, Michelle (2007). 'Review of Richard Kraut, What is Good and Why: The Ethics of Well-Being '. *Notre Dame Philosophical Reviews*, 11. https://ndpr.nd.edu/news/23251-what-is-good-and-why-the-ethics-of-well-being, accessed 22 December 2015.

Sher, George (1997). *Beyond Neutrality* (Cambridge University Press).

5   The happiness theory of well-being

5.1 Introduction

So far we have examined hedonism, desire-fulfilment theory, objective list theory and perfectionism. In this chapter we will look at another theory of well-being: the happiness theory of well-being (HTWB). My overall aim is to assess this theory of well-being. My means of doing so is to assess the theory when we combine it with various theories of the nature of happiness. Thus in this chapter we will spend time examining the major theories of the nature of happiness.

Before getting started properly, we need to be aware of a terminological difficulty. The term 'happiness' is deployed in a wide variety of ways across ancient philosophy, psychology, welfare economics and contemporary philosophy. One very problematic use of the term 'happiness' is simply as a way of referring to well-being. That is, some people treat 'well-being' and 'happiness' as two ways of referring to the same thing and use the two terms interchangeably (they might also do the same with 'utility').[1] We see this in passages such as:

> I take the terms well-being, utility, happiness, life satisfaction, and welfare to be interchangeable[.][2]

According to this way of using the word 'happiness', each of the theories of well-being we have examined so far in this book are necessarily theories of happiness. One major problem with that way of using the term 'happiness' is that it immediately closes a collection of philosophical questions. These include:

i   Does happiness contribute to well-being, does it have any prudential value?
ii Is happiness the sole prudential value, the only thing that contributes to well-being?
iii Does unhappiness reduce well-being, does it have prudential disvalue?
iv Is unhappiness the sole prudential disvalue, the only thing that reduces well-being?

To see that these are real philosophical questions, imagine someone who held the following views. The first is a view about what happiness *is*:

> **Pleasure theory of happiness (PTH)**: To be happy *just is* to have a high hedonic level. To be unhappy *just is* to have a low hedonic level.

The second is a view about well-being:

> **Desire-fulfilment theory of well-being**: Something is non-instrumentally good for you if and only if and because it fulfils a non-instrumental desire of yours. Something is non-instrumentally bad for you if and only if and because it frustrates a non-instrumental desire of yours.

According to a person who holds these views, there is such a thing as happiness (it consists in having a high hedonic level). But according to this person, someone's level of happiness and their level of well-being can diverge. This is because someone might (a) fail to desire happiness or (b) desire things other than happiness. Thus, according to this combination of views, some happiness might not contribute to well-being (happiness that is not desired) and some things other than happiness contribute to well-being (things that are distinct from happiness and that fulfil the agent's desires).

Here is a second example, to demonstrate the point. Suppose someone held this combination of views:

> **Pleasure theory of happiness and unhappiness**: To be happy *just is* to have a high hedonic level. To be unhappy *just is* to have a low hedonic level.

> **Well-being perfectionism**: What is non-instrumentally good or bad for a human is determined by human nature. The exercise and development of the capacities essential to humans conditioned on their being living things is good for humans. The diminishment of the capacities essential to humans conditioned on their being living things is bad for humans.

Could someone holding both these views think that happiness and well-being diverge? Yes. Here is how. They might think that happiness is not one of the relevant capacities (e.g. those essential to humans conditioned on being living things). For that reason they might think that happiness is *never* non-instrumentally good for us (and that unhappiness is never non-instrumentally bad for us).

Leave aside the question of how *plausible* these combinations of views are. Even if they are false we can still learn something from the possibility of someone holding such views. Someone who held one of these combinations of views does not seem to be confused about the meaning of the words 'happiness' or 'well-being'. But if 'happiness' and 'well-being' are synonymous then the person who has one of the pairs of views just described would be completely confused.[3]

What is the upshot of this? The important point is that we should not casually treat 'happiness' and 'well-being' as synonyms. A number of theories of well-being allow well-being to come apart from anything that could plausibly be called happiness. For this reason we should be sure to only use 'happiness' to refer to that particular thing (be it a psychological state or something else) and we should treat as a serious philosophical question whether happiness and well-being are connected in some way.

There is at least one more complication in the way that the terms 'happy' and 'happiness' are used that we should be careful of. This can be seen in the difference between:

1   Nisha is happy.
2   Nisha is a happy person.
3   Nisha is happy that the prowler has been arrested/that interest rates are going up.

These claims are not obviously attributing the same kind of thing to Nisha (notice that it seems like one of them could be true without the others being true).

We might think that the third claim attributes something like being *pleased that* some outcome has occurred or *satisfied with* some outcome. But this seems distinct from being *happy* in the sense attributed by the first claim. For it seems that even if one is unhappy one can still be pleased or satisfied that various things are the case. A clear example of this is when something very bad happens to you and you hear that the culprit has been arrested. Does this make you *happy*? Not clearly. Though you might be pleased that someone has been arrested.

What of the difference between the first and second claims? Here the difference seems less stark. The second claim plausibly attributes a *disposition* or tendency towards the state of being happy. This disposition need not be exceptionless – a happy person is not someone who is *always* happy. Rather, they are someone likely to be happy across a wide range of circumstances. (For comparison: 'He's funny.'). They are highly disposed to be happy. And the happiness they are disposed to is plausibly that which is attributed in the first claim.

The relation between the first and second ways of using 'happy' is not problematic. The first attributes a certain kind of state to a person. The second attributes a disposition of the person to being in that state. As for the third claim and its ilk – 'happy that P' claims – there are a range of different options. Option 1 is to think that being happy *that*/pleased *that* is a form of pleasure (distinct from but no less of a pleasure than sensory pleasure). Option 2 is to treat being happy that/pleased that as distinct from pleasure. Option 1 would give a more inclusive conception of pleasure with which to formulate pleasure theories of happiness. Option 2 treats these states as distinct from pleasure, and thus irrelevant to pleasure theories of happiness (but possibly relevant to other theories of happiness).

5.2 Three views about happiness and well-being

Having distinguished happiness and well-being let us consider some of the possible views that one might have about their relation. In particular, it will be useful to think about what each of the different theories of well-being implies about the relation between happiness and well-being.

There are at least four views of the relation between happiness and well-being we might have:

1   Happiness *alone* is non-instrumentally good for us.
2   Happiness is one of a *plurality* of things that is non-instrumentally good for us.
3   Happiness is sometimes non-instrumentally good for us but sometimes not.
4   Happiness is never non-instrumentally good for us.

Who might hold each of these possible views?[4]

The fourth view might be held by hedonists (so long as they think that happiness is wholly distinct from pleasure). It will also be held by any objective list theorist who denies that happiness is one of the goods on the list. It might also be held by those perfectionists, if they think that happiness is not one of the relevant human capacities.

The third view might be held by some desire-fulfilment theorists. Such desire-fulfilment theorists would think that some people desire happiness but that some do not. Thus some happiness is prudentially valuable whilst some is not.[5]

The second view will be held by objective list theorists who include happiness as one of the goods on the list, among others.

The first view claims that happiness alone contributes to well-being. This will be held by someone who subscribes to the happiness theory of well-being, the main topic of this chapter. Let us formulate this theory as follows:

The happiness theory of well-being

*   All and only happiness is non-instrumentally good for us.
*   All and only unhappiness is non-instrumentally bad for us.
*   A person's overall level of well-being (at some particular time, or over some period) is determined solely by their overall level of happiness.

(Henceforth I often omit the 'non-instrumentally', for the sake of readability. All claims about what is good for should be taken to be about what is non-instrumentally good for, unless otherwise specified.)

To assess the plausibility of the happiness theory of well-being we will need to know what happiness *is*. Let us therefore look at the candidate theories of happiness.

In addition to helping us to get closer to the truth about the nature of happiness, examining these theories will enable us to achieve two further tasks simultaneously. The main thing it will achieve is that of helping us to assess the happiness theory of well-being. The second thing that it will achieve is that of helping us to assess the plausibility of the second view above, that happiness – but not only happiness – has prudential value. Thus the questions that we should be asking as we assess the theories of happiness are:

a   Is this a plausible theory of happiness in its own right? Does it get happiness right?
b   If we plug this theory of happiness into the happiness theory of well-being how plausible is the resulting view?
c   If we assume this theory of happiness, how plausible is it that happiness has prudential value at all (even if it is not the only prudential value)?

5.3 The nature of happiness (1): pleasure theories of happiness

Our first candidate theory of happiness was that introduced above, the pleasure theory of happiness. This is the view that being happy just is having a certain balance of pleasure over pain. This need not be restricted to sensory pain and pleasure but can encompass any kinds of pleasure and pain. Using the idea of a hedonic level introduced earlier,[6] we can formulate the pleasure theory of happiness as follows:

> **Pleasure theory of happiness**: To be happy *just is* to have a hedonic level of H or above. To be unhappy *just is* to have a hedonic level of U or below.[7]

There are quite a few questions that such a definition leaves open. First is the question of the nature of pleasure (this came up above in relation to claims like 'S is happy that P'). But let us bracket that question.

A more pressing issue is that the pleasure theory of happiness just formulated makes reference to thresholds (H, U) in someone's hedonic levels as the thresholds where they are happy/unhappy. This makes pressing the question of where these thresholds for happiness and unhappiness are. Answering this question is not straightforward.

Here is a first proposal. Suppose that H and U are identified with very high and very low hedonic levels. The sorts of limits that we reach only during extreme pleasure or pain.

Note that one consequence of this theory of happiness is that there will be a large region – from just under the 'happy' boundary to just above the 'unhappy' boundary – in which the person will be neither happy nor unhappy (between points H and U):

(H)appy	*POINT H*
Neither happy nor unhappy	
Neither happy nor unhappy	
Neither happy nor unhappy	
Neither happy nor unhappy	
Hedonic Neutrality	
Neither happy nor unhappy	
Neither happy nor unhappy	
Neither happy nor unhappy	
Neither happy nor unhappy	
(U)nhappy	*POINT U*

One might find that implausible given the very large differences in hedonic level between Point H and Point U. It seems implausible and to fit poorly with the general idea of a pleasure theory of happiness to allow the point immediately above U to both be classed as simply 'neither happy nor unhappy' given the degree of difference between them.

If one thinks that this is a problematic consequence of that pleasure theory of happiness and unhappiness, one might prefer instead to adopt the view that H is the minimal degree above neutrality and U is the minimal distance below hedonic neutrality. On this way of setting H and U, to be happy *just is* to have a positive hedonic level and to be unhappy *just is* to have a negative hedonic level.

This proposal for the happiness and unhappiness boundaries avoids the problem above. It does this by reducing the 'neither happy nor unhappy' region to the narrowest of bands – just hedonic neutrality. We can represent this thus:

Happy	
Happy	
Happy	
Happy	
Happy	
Happy	*POINT H*
Hedonic Neutrality	Neither happy nor unhappy

Unhappy	*POINT U*
Unhappy	
Unhappy	
Unhappy	
Unhappy	
Unhappy	

Is this a better proposal for PTH to adopt?

One might have exactly the opposite worry for this form of the pleasure theory of happiness from the one aired above. More precisely, one might have two worries:

1   It sets the boundary for happiness too low.
2   The difference between Point H and Point U is now too *small* to be the difference between being *happy* and being *unhappy*.

To illustrate these points consider the following scenario. Suppose someone is sitting in a waiting room listening to a mildly pleasant piece of music. Their hedonic level is very slightly above hedonic neutrality. According to the current proposal for the happiness and unhappiness boundaries the person in this situation is necessarily *happy*. One might worry that this is to underestimate *how good* one must feel in order to be happy.

Now, suppose that one then experiences a slightly painful calf cramp such that one's hedonic level moves to very marginally *below* hedonic neutrality. If the current view were true then this transition would necessarily be a transition from being *happy* to being *unhappy*. A few seconds ago you were happy. Now you are unhappy. But one might worry that that seems too big a change to result from such a *small* change in hedonic level.

The upshot of these points is that a pleasure theory of happiness needs to determine the boundaries for happiness and unhappiness in such a way that the gap between point H and point U is neither too small nor too large. It should also provide a plausible account of when one is happy (arguably, one that requires that one be more than minimally above hedonic neutrality). A major question for a pleasure theory of happiness is how exactly to answer that question, how to achieve that balance.

The previous issue was relevant to the question of the *general adequacy* of the pleasure theory of happiness, the question of whether it gets happiness right. What else can we say about the general adequacy of the pleasure theory of happiness?

One positive feature of the view is that it nicely explains why being in significant pain tends to coincide with being unhappy. For if being unhappy just is to be at a hedonic level below a certain point then someone in significant pain is thereby unhappy.

Another plausible feature of the pleasure theory of happiness is that it would nicely explain our tendency to think that we are each authoritative (at least generally) with respect to whether we are happy. If my being happy is explained entirely by my being at a certain hedonic level then, given the plausible assumption that I am generally authoritative as to whether I am experiencing pleasure or pain, I am authoritative as to whether I am happy.

A question for the pleasure theory of happiness is whether it allows too wide a class of things to count as happy. Take the set of creatures that can feel pleasure, is it plausible to think that all of them can be happy? This is not so obvious. For example, whilst a dog or a cat can experience pleasure some will be reluctant to think that such animals are capable of *happiness*. One explanation that might be offered is that happiness involves something cognitive and complex – a kind of judgement about one's life as a whole – and that these kinds of judgements are too sophisticated to ascribe to cats and dogs (for example).

There is much more to say on all of these issues. However, I think that it makes sense to move on to seeing what results from combining the pleasure theory of happiness with the happiness theory of well-being. Here is a reminder of the two views:

> **Pleasure theory of happiness**: To be happy *just is* to have a hedonic level H or higher. To be unhappy *just is* to have a negative hedonic level U or lower.

> **The happiness theory of well-being:** All and only happiness is non-instrumentally good for us. All and only unhappiness is non-instrumentally bad for us. A person's overall level of well-being (at some particular time, or in some duration) is determined solely by their overall level of happiness.

This combination of views is only slightly different from the view we examined in chapter 1, namely hedonism about well-being. For that reason, it seems like it will inherit the upsides and the downsides of that view.

One of the main objections to hedonism about well-being was that, in cases like Nozick's experience machine, the view is committed to the claim that a life in the experience machine at some hedonic level is *necessarily* equal in prudential value to a life outside the machine at the same level whatever else is true of the life outside the machine (that it contains friendships, achievements, etc.). Clearly, this combination (happiness theory of well-being plus the pleasure theory of happiness) will generate the same result. According to HTWB and PTH, if one is at a certain hedonic level then one is *necessarily* at a certain happiness level and level of well-being. Everyone at the same hedonic level necessarily has the same level of happiness and therefore of well-being. And this will be true irrespective of whether that hedonic level is inside the experience machine or outside of it. Thus the experience machine objection applies equally to this view as to hedonism.

In a similar fashion, the objection to hedonism that it allows malicious plea-sures and other kinds of problematic pleasures to contribute to well-being will have the same force against HTWB and PTH as this theory must also say that malicious pleasures are prudentially valuable. Thus this combination of views will be vulnerable or immune from this charge to the same extent that hedonism is.

Comparative merits?

We have just seen that HTWB and PTH will overlap with hedonism about well-being for the most part. For that reason it will be vulnerable to the same objections and have the same kinds of merits that hedonism has. That might make us worry that it will either be difficult (or unimportant) to decide between the two views. This is not quite right, however. Hedonism about well-being might have advantages over this combination of HTWB and PTH.

Remember that the pleasure theory of happiness needs to determine the boundaries for H and U, which are the hedonic levels where someone is happy or unhappy respectively. We considered above a proposal that set H and U very high. One consequence of this way of setting H and U is that HTWB and PTH will ascribe prudential value (PV) to a smaller range of positive hedonic levels than hedonism does. We can represent this thus:

Table 5.1

HEDONIC LEVEL	HTWB & PTH	Hedonism
(H)appy	PV	PV
Neither happy nor unhappy	No PV	PV
Neither happy nor unhappy	No PV	PV
Neither happy nor unhappy	No PV	PV
Neither happy nor unhappy	No PV	PV
Neither happy nor unhappy	No PV	PV
Hedonic Neutrality		

HTWB and PTH ascribe prudential value to happiness alone. On this construal of PTH, where H is set much higher than hedonic neutrality, only some positive hedonic levels constitute happiness and have prudential value. One consequence of this is that a wide range of hedonic levels that hedonism ascribes prudential value to are given zero prudential value by HTWB and PTH. Moreover, HTWB and PTH ascribe the same prudential value to all hedonic levels between H and U, which seems implausible.

As we saw earlier, one way for HTWB and PTH to avoid these problematic results is to instead adopt the view that H and U are marginally above and below hedonic neutrality. One consequence of this is that HTWB and PTH will then generate the exact same verdicts as hedonism about well-being. (This is because all hedonic levels above neutrality will be ones where the agent is happy, according to this view.)

The downside to going this way is the issue we saw above. This way of setting H and U arguably reduces the plausibility of PTH *as an account of happiness*. It does not seem very plausible that every hedonic level above neutrality is one where the agent is *happy* (and vice versa for hedonic levels below neutrality, not all of those seem necessarily to be ones where an agent is *unhappy*). It makes the distance between happiness and unhappiness too small, as we saw in the case above.

The upshot of this is a dilemma for HTWB and PTH. Unlike hedonism about well-being it must supply an account of where the thresholds for happiness (and thus prudential value) occur. But either:

(horn 1) it sets the boundaries high, in which case it ascribes equal (zero) prudential value to a wide range of hedonic levels

OR

(horn 2) it sets the boundaries low, in which case it generates the same verdicts as hedonism but possibly at the expense of undermining the plausibility of its theory of happiness.

Even if HTWB and PTH match hedonism's verdicts about all cases that does not result in a tie between the two views. For the assessment of a view is sensitive to more than the implications it generates for particular cases. HTWB and PTH incurs and a substantive commitment about the nature of happiness, one that hedonism does not incur. This leaves HTWB and PTH vulnerable if its theory of happiness is implausible, as I have suggested that it may be. For this reason I think we should conclude in answer to the main guiding question of this chapter that hedonism about well-being is likely more plausible than the following combination: the happiness theory of well-being *combined with the pleasure theory of happiness*.

Have we rejected the pleasure theory of happiness?

Keep in mind that in this section we have been assessing the happiness theory of well-being in conjunction with the pleasure theory of happiness in order to assess the happiness theory of well-being. Our main interest was in the resulting combination of views, not the pleasure theory of happiness in particular.

I have argued that the happiness theory of well-being, when combined with the pleasure theory of happiness, is weaker than hedonism about well-being.

But notice that the view that happiness and unhappiness *just is* being above and below particular hedonic levels was not deemed to be problematic in its own right. The problem was in *combining* that view with the happiness theory of well-being – because it meant that a wide range of hedonic levels have to be ascribed the same (zero) degree of prudential value.

If a pleasure theory of happiness is correct it is not clear that happiness is a distinct prudential good, aside from pleasure. For example, any objective list theory with pleasure on the list would seem to generate the same results whether or not it has happiness on the list as well. (One might also worry about double-counting.) There is no obvious need for an objective list theory of well-being to incorporate both pleasure and happiness, if a pleasure theory of happiness is true.

We have not here rejected the pleasure theory of happiness in its own right. Whether it is generally adequate is not a question we can hope to fully address in this chapter. But certainly for the reasons given above, a pleasure theory of happiness seems more plausible if it treats H and U as being significantly above hedonic neutrality. That way we do not get the problem of small changes in hedonic level necessarily meaning that an agent has gone from being happy to being unhappy.

5.4 The nature of happiness (2): life satisfaction theories of happiness

The view we have just considered married the happiness theory of well-being with a pleasure theory of happiness. One alternative we should consider now is that of replacing the pleasure theory of happiness with a *life satisfaction theory of happiness.*

Life satisfaction theories of happiness (LSH) are widely held within psychology and economics. Such theories take happiness to be identical to the state of being satisfied with your life. This is interpreted in terms of making a certain kind of positive judgement about your life as a whole. We can present a generic life satisfaction theory of happiness thus:

> **Life satisfaction theory of happiness**: One's degree of happiness is one's degree of satisfaction with one's life as a whole. To be happy *just is* to be satisfied with your life as a whole. To be unhappy *just is* to be unsatisfied with your life as a whole.

Remember that, as with the pleasure theory of happiness, we are interested primarily in the combination of LSH plus the happiness theory of well-being.

LSH as formulated above leaves a number of questions to be answered. Some of these do not have easy answers, at least when we combine LSH with HWB. Here is one: What is the relevant judgement when it comes to life satisfaction?[8]

Different LSH theories will have different accounts of what exactly the relevant judgement is. And we might wonder what exactly the relevant judgement is supposed to be. Put another way, *what* am I being asked when I asked whether I am satisfied with my life as a whole? To see the difficulty this question generates, suppose we start with this case:

> **Undecided Ursula**: Ursula lives a life full of enjoyable pursuits. She has many friends, she is successful in her career as a pilot and she has an active social life full of hobbies and fun. One day a psychologist, seeking to determine her level of happiness, asks her to rate 'how satisfied she is with her life as a whole' by choosing a point on a scale from very satisfied to very unsatisfied. Ursula replies: 'I don't understand the question. There are lots of ways of evaluating my life. Can you clarify?'

What should the psychologist say to Ursula to help her to answer the question? The problem arises because there are lots of ways of interpreting 'satisfaction with your life as a whole'. Imagine these four ways that the psychologist could answer:

1   **Meaningfulness**: whether you are satisfied with your life as a whole is a matter of how meaningful you judge it to be.
2   **Life plan fit**: whether you are satisfied with your life as a whole is a matter of how closely it approximates your life plan.
3   **Enjoyment**: whether you are satisfied with your life as a whole is a matter of how much you enjoy its constituent elements.
4   **Hold fixed**: whether you are satisfied with your life as a whole is a matter of how much change you would make to it, if you could (with more change indicating less satisfaction and vice versa).

The problem now is that the answers to these different ways of interpreting the question 'how satisfied are you with your life as a whole?' might diverge. Suppose Ursula gives the following answers, depending on which clarification the psychologist provides:

> **Ursula 1**: 'In that case I am moderately unsatisfied with my life as a whole. I greatly enjoy it but I do not think that much that I do has much meaning. After all, it's not as if I am campaigning for social justice or finding a cure for cancer. I enjoy what I do but it does not matter much in the grand scheme of things.'

> **Ursula 2**: 'In that case I am moderately satisfied with my life as a whole. My whole life I wanted to be a psychiatrist. But once I qualified I hated it. I also intended to have children but I never met anyone I could have children with. However, I always wanted to be a pilot. I didn't think it would be my full time job (though I am very glad it is). And I always wanted to be a rock climber, gardener, and hockey player, which I am.'

Ursula 3: 'In that case I am very satisfied with my life as a whole. I enjoy all aspects of it greatly.'

Ursula 4: 'In that case I am very unsatisfied with my life as a whole. If I could, I would change my life so that I had had children. That would have meant doing a different job and I wouldn't have lived where I do now, not with a family. Nor would I want to have so many hobbies, not if I'd had children.'

I take it that Ursula's answers in each of these cases 1–4 are both (a) answers that she could plausibly and candidly give in answer to the psychologist's clarification of the question and (b) very different. After all, across these ways of clarifying the question, her answers range from 'very satisfied' to 'very unsatisfied'. The question then is as follows: *which* of these is the judgement that is important for LSH? Which of these judgements tells us her level of happiness, if any?

One reply that the LSH theorist might make is to argue that *one* of 1–4 is the relevant judgement. They might say (for example) that the meaningfulness judgement is the relevant judgement. One problem for that is that it does not seem so obvious that our degree of happiness is necessarily identical to our degree of satisfaction on each of these dimensions. To give some examples, it seems perfectly coherent for someone to report being unhappy despite judging their life to be meaningful, or to fit with their life plan. Indeed, they might say: 'I know that my life has gone exactly as I want it to. But I'm not *happy*.' And the same seems to be true for at least judgements of meaningfulness ('My life is important and meaningful. But I'm not *happy*.') and degree of change ('I wouldn't change much about my life. But I'm not *happy*.')

Suppose that this is right, such that we cannot identify happiness with one's degree of satisfaction along one of these dimensions. Here is another reply the LSH theorist might make. They might reject the idea that any of these particular judgements above is the one that constitutes Ursula's level of happiness. Instead, the LSH theorist might urge that LSH judgements are supposed to be *global* and so the relevant judgement is an *overall* judgement, one that encompasses all (or perhaps only some) of the judgements identified above. Does that help? Not clearly, for it seems to generate three problems.

Problem 1: Which judgements?

Presumably not *every* possible way that someone could positively evaluate their life is constitutive of happiness. (For example, some might dispute whether judgements of *meaningfulness* are relevant.) Thus the LSH theorist must provide *some* account of which domains of judgement go into the global judgement that the LSH view identifies with a person's degree of happiness. This is not an objection to the view but shows that there is work to do in developing it to sufficient detail to examine it.

Problem 2: Uncertainty

Here is a reply that Ursula might make to this latest suggestion: 'I can make each of the judgements identified above – judgements of meaningfulness, life plan fit, enjoyment, amount I would change my life. But I have no idea how to put these together as a whole. I do not know what my *overall* degree of satisfaction is, putting together all of these judgements.'

This seems like a perfectly understandable reply. Certainly it does not seem easy to move from these local kinds of judgements to an *overall* level of satisfaction. Replies like Ursula's might be common, or at least possible. But given the detail of the LSH view, Ursula's being undecided here means that she is not happy or unhappy (after all she does not have any judgement about her overall degree of satisfaction). But that does not seem particularly plausible. A person's inability to make this judgement seems perfectly compatible with their being happy or unhappy.

Problem 3: Satisfaction: cognitive or affective?

A further problem arises from thinking about how complicated life-satisfaction judgements are. Ursula, we are imagining, is asked to make one of these judgements and, in trying to, has the opportunity to ask follow-up questions of the psychologist. But the LSH theory is supposed to be the correct theory of happiness *generally*. Remember that it holds that one's degree of happiness is identical to one's degree of satisfaction with one's life. (To be happy just is to judge oneself satisfied with one's life as a whole.)

One problem for this is that anyone who does not make such a judgement is, according to LSH, not happy. But it does not seem plausible to think that *everyone* who has *ever* been happy or unhappy to some degree has held one of these global satisfaction beliefs. Given how demanding such a judgement is supposed to be – it is supposed encompass a number of relevant ways of evaluating your life – it seems that this version of LSH generates the result that many apparently happy and unhappy people are not so, because they have not made quite a detached, complicated, intellectual judgement about their life.

One point that this brings out is that so far we have interpreted LSH's satisfaction judgements *cognitively* – that one's degree of satisfaction with one's life as a whole is a *belief* about one's life. Maybe that is a mistake. Perhaps one's degree of satisfaction with one's life as a whole is better understood *affectively*, a matter of how one *feels* about one's life.

Would this make LSH more plausible? Seemingly so. First, as we saw above, Ursula could have all sorts of sincere beliefs about her life and how well she is doing along various dimensions whilst truthfully reporting that she is not happy. Making the relevant kind of satisfaction a feeling would likely avoid this problem. Second, it seems more plausible that everyone who is happy or unhappy has some degree of overall positive or negative feeling about their life as a whole rather than having some *belief* about their life as a whole. Let us suppose then that LSH is best formulated thus:

> **Life satisfaction theory of happiness (LSH) 2**: One's degree of happiness is one's degree of felt satisfaction with one's life as a whole. To be happy just is to feel satisfied with your life as a whole. To be unhappy just is to feel unsatisfied with your life as a whole.

Suppose that this is the best form of LSH. Now let us return to our guiding question: how plausible is a happiness theory of well-being when combined with LSH2? Remember that the happiness theory of well-being is as follows:

> **The happiness theory of well-being:** All and only happiness is non-instrumentally good for us. All and only unhappiness is non-instrumentally bad for us. A person's overall level of well-being (at some particular time, or in some duration) is determined solely by their overall level of happiness.

5.5 Problems for LSH2 plus the happiness theory of well-being

(1) Does it collapse LSH2 into the pleasure theory of happiness?

One consequence of holding a form of LSH that takes the agent's *felt* satisfaction with their life to be constitutive of happiness is that the difference between the LSH and the *hedonic* theory of happiness becomes quite small. Essentially, the only times that the views differ in the claims they make will be in cases of pleasure that are *not* also feelings of satisfaction with one's life. Such pleasures are not constitutive of happiness, according to *LSH*, but they are constitutive of happiness, according to a *hedonic* theory of happiness.

When we combine LSH2 with the happiness theory of well-being, we get the result that any pleasure or other positive feeling that is not a feeling of satisfaction with one's own life will have no (non-instrumental) prudential value and any pain or other negative feeling will have no (non-instrumental) prudential disvalue. This generates a dilemma for LSH2+Happiness theory of well-being. We can see this from the following case:

> **Undecided Ursula continues her day:** Having finished talking to the psychologist, Ursula continues her day. She has an exquisite, enjoyable, lunch. She drinks some wonderful beer which she gets great pleasure from. She plays ping pong

with people at the bar. She then walks along the beach back home. When she gets home a migraine strikes. She has a horrible headache and feels pretty wretched. She decides to go and buy some painkillers. But on her way out the house she slips down the front stairs, breaking her finger. Fifteen minutes later she is discovered by a neighbour who gets her to hospital.

Ursula enjoys a number of pleasurable experiences followed by some painful ones. The trouble for the LSH2 + Happiness theory of well-being is that, on one plausible reading of LSH2, these experiences have no prudential value or disvalue. When Ursula is having a fun time it is not obvious that all of the pleasurable experiences count as feelings of satisfaction *with her life*. Conversely, the pain that she experiences during the migraine and her accident are not obviously feelings of dissatisfaction with her life. She is in pain but she has not changed her feelings about her life. Thus on one reading of LSH2 + Happiness theory of well-being, none of these experiences have prudential value or disvalue for Ursula. But that seems implausible. These experiences are bad for someone, even if they do not change their feelings about their life as a whole.

A natural reply for LSH2 + Happiness theory of well-being is to claim that all of Ursula's pleasure and pains in the example in fact *are* feelings of satisfaction and dissatisfaction with Ursula's life. They might say: 'when she enjoys the beer she is satisfied that her life is one that contains this experience. And when she has the painful accident she is dissatisfied with her life for containing this pain.'

This might be right. But the trouble with this reply is that it risks collapsing LSH2 into the hedonic theory of happiness. If all pleasures no matter how sensory their nature are necessarily a form of satisfaction with one's life then LSH2 and the hedonic theory of happiness seem to be one and the same view, so there is only one theory of happiness here not two. This, in turn, would mean that LSH2 + the happiness theory of well-being is not a *distinct* option.

It is unclear which way the LSH2 + happiness theory of well-being should go here. On the one hand they can 'bite the bullet' by allowing that not all pleasures and pains necessarily are (or generate) feelings of satisfaction or dissatisfaction with one's life. But that seems problematic because some of the pains and pleasures that will be omitted seem like plausible candidates for prudential value and disvalue (pleasures and pains like Ursula experiences). On the other hand they can have an expansive idea of 'feelings of satisfaction with one's life'. That prevents the happiness theory of well-being from getting implausible results. But it risks collapsing LSH2 into hedonism about well-being.

Here is the dilemma:

(horn 1) Either some pleasures are *not* feelings of satisfaction with one's own life.[9]

OR

(horn 2) All pleasures just are feelings of satisfaction with one's own life.

If the LSH2 + happiness theory of well-being takes horn 1 it must say that such pleasures and pains do not contribute to well-being. If it takes horn 2 then the view seems identical to hedonism. Thus the LSH2 + happiness theory of well-being is either (a) less plausible than hedonism OR (b) identical to it.

(2) Experience machine

As with the combination of the hedonic theory of happiness + the happiness theory of well-being, the combination of LSH + the happiness theory of well-being is also vulnerable to the experience machine objection. This is because one could easily be highly satisfied with a life based on false beliefs and experiences (perhaps it would have to be unbeknownst to you that they were false beliefs and experiences). And the happiness theory of well-being ascribes prudential value to no goods other than happiness. Thus, like hedonism, LSH + the happiness theory of well-being is forced to conclude that any two people whose levels of life satisfaction are identical will have identical levels of well-being. To the extent that we reject hedonism on account of its being vulnerable to the experience machine we thus have no reason to prefer the happiness theory of well-being, at least when combined with LSH.

(3) Extreme satisfaction

Another kind of problem for LSH + Happiness theory of well-being comes from people who are very easily satisfied. Take this case:

> **Satisfied Sunita**: Sunita suffers from a range of severe mental and physical disabilities. Her condition means that she rarely leaves the house. She has no hobbies or interests nor does she have any friends. She spends her time watching gameshows.

Suppose now that Sunita is given an experimental new drug. The drug does not alleviate any of her disabilities. But it does have an odd side-effect; it makes her *extremely* satisfied with her life. (Depending on the form of LSH this will either be a belief or a feeling.) Suppose that she is intensely satisfied with her life. According to LSH + Happiness theory of well-being Sunita's life is now going extremely *well*. After all, she is extremely satisfied with her life. This entails that she is extremely happy. And this entails that she has a very high level of well-being. But this seems implausible. Of course, it might be true that this side-effect is good for Sunita, it makes her situation *better* than it was. But it does not plausibly give her an extremely *high* level of well-being. This casts doubt on the LSH + Happiness theory of well-being. Whilst satisfaction might be good for someone, it seems that there is more to well-being than simply their degree of satisfaction.[10]

5.6 Conclusion

In this chapter we have examined the happiness theory of well-being. To do this we have examined two prominent theories of happiness – the pleasure theory of happiness and the life-satisfaction theory of happiness. From what we have seen there is little to recommend a happiness theory of well-being over hedonism when combined with either of these theories of happiness.

A big question then is whether there is some *other* theory of happiness that can simultaneously achieve two things:

1   Provide a generally plausible account of happiness
2   Yield a form of the happiness theory of well-being that is distinct from and more plausible than hedonism about well-being.

Rather than examine any more theories of happiness let me just mention two. First, one could adopt a *hybrid* theory of happiness.[11] One such hybrid theory would take happiness to be a combination of pleasure *and* satisfaction with one's life as a whole. Another kind of theory of happiness, one recently defended by Dan Haybron, identifies happiness with one's overall *emotional condition*.

One of these might be the correct theory of happiness. But from what we have seen so far I think that we should be doubtful that either is going to yield a happiness theory of well-being that is more plausible than hedonism about well-being. This is for two reasons.

First, in order not to collapse into hedonism about well-being, a happiness theory of well-being needs a theory of happiness and unhappiness in which they are distinct from pleasure and pain. But this will lead such a theory of well-being to give problematic verdicts about pleasures and pains in cases like Ursula's (or other cases of pleasures and pains not constitutive of happiness). It will be forced to say of such pleasures and pains that they have no prudential value or disvalue. Thus the pressure not to collapse into hedonism will force the theory into giving problematic answers about some pleasures and pains.

Second, any plausible theory of happiness is going to generate the result that the happiness theory of well-being is just as vulnerable to the experience machine objection as hedonism is. Given that this is a major objection to hedonism, it is problematic that the happiness theory of well-being will be equally vulnerable.

The weak point here is the happiness theory of well-being. *None* of the theories of *happiness* mentioned in this chapter has been rejected. Any one of them may be the truth about happiness. The problem comes from combining them with the happiness theory of well-being. This is because the happiness theory of well-being can only remain distinct from hedonism about well-being by committing itself to problematic consequences about pleasures and pains in some cases (namely that they are not prudentially valuable or disvaluable). In light of this

I think that we should judge that a happiness theory of well-being either collapses into hedonism or is no more plausible (and possibly less plausible) than hedonism.

Nothing in this chapter has shown that happiness might not have prudential value. If happiness is distinct from pleasure then it still seems like something that has some prudential value. After all, in the case of satisfied Sunita, it certainly seems like becoming extremely satisfied with her life had *some* prudential value, even if it was not enough to necessarily give her a high level of well-being. So from what we have seen in the major theories of happiness it might be that happiness holds prudential value even if it is not the *only* thing that holds prudential value.

Comprehension questions

1   What different things might be meant by the claim that someone is satisfied with their life?
2   Why is Undecided Ursula's accident a problem for the combination of LSH2 and a Happiness theory of well-being?
3   What might a life-satisfaction judgement be?

Further questions

(1)   Is some sort of hybrid theory of happiness plausible?
(2)   Would a hybrid theory of happiness yield a more plausible happiness theory of well-being?

Notes

1 Mill (1863). Another example is the pairing of a newspaper headline, 'David Cameron aims to make happiness the new GDP', with a story about the government focusing on well-being: 'If low levels of wellbeing can be shown to be correlated with areas particularly hit by the government's programme of cuts, then the ramifications are obvious – but some in government appear to want to know rather than guess.' http://www.theguardian.com/politics/2010/nov/14/david-cameron-well being-inquiry, accessed 22 December 2015.
2 Easterlin (2005: 29).
3 For the use of this kind of argument elsewhere in practical philosophy, see Moore (1903).
4 The range of answers given here is not exhaustive.
5 Things will vary greatly between different desire-fulfilment theorists. Others might hold that necessarily all humans desire happiness. In that case, if the view were true, all happiness would have prudential value.
6 See chapter 1.
7 See e.g. Mill (1863). 'By happiness is intended pleasure, and the absence of pain; by unhappiness, pain, and the privation of pleasure.'
8 You might think that this is a mistake and that the relevant kind of satisfaction is affective (a feeling) rather than cognitive (a judgement). I discuss that possibility shortly.
9 One possibility suggested by these issues is a more complicated theory of happiness, one that takes pleasure *and* life-satisfaction to contribute to happiness. This would allow a happiness theory of well-being that incorporated this theory of happiness to give different verdicts from hedonism.

10 For extensive further discussion see Haybron (2008: chapter 5).
11 Not to be confused with a hybrid theory of well-being (see chapter 6).

References

Easterlin, R. A. (2005). 'Building a Better Theory of Well-being' in L. Bruni and P. L. Porta (eds.), *Economics and Happiness: Framing the Analysis* (Oxford University Press).
Moore, G. E. (1903). *Principia Ethica.*

Happiness and well-being

Badhwar, Neera K. (2014). *Well-Being: Happiness in a Worthwhile Life* (Oxford University Press).
Bloomfield, Paul (2014). *The Virtues of Happiness: A Theory of the Good Life* (Oxford University Press).
Mill, J. S. (1863). *Utilitarianism.*
Raibley, Jason R. (2012). 'Happiness is not Well-Being'. *Journal of Happiness Studies*, 13(6): 1105–1129.
Sumner, L. W. (1996). *Welfare, Happiness, and Ethics* (Oxford University Press).

Theories of happiness

Feldman, Fred (2010). *What is This Thing Called Happiness?* (Oxford University Press).
Haybron, Daniel M. (2003). 'What Do We Want from a Theory of Happiness?' *Metaphilosophy*, 34(3): 305–329.
Haybron, Daniel M. (2008). *The Pursuit of Unhappiness: The Elusive Psychology of Well-Being* (Oxford University Press).
Kahneman, Daniel (1999). 'Objective Happiness' in D. Kahneman, E. Diener and N. Schwarz (eds.), *Well-Being: Foundations of Hedonic Psychology* (Russell Sage Foundation).
Suikkanen, Jussi (2011). 'An Improved Whole Life Satisfaction Theory of Happiness'. *International Journal of Wellbeing*, 1(1): 149–166.

Issues in measurement of happiness, happiness and psychology

Alexandrova, Anna (2008). 'First-Person Reports and the Measurement of Happiness'. *Philosophical Psychology*, 21(5): 571–583.
Angner, Erik (2013). 'Is it Possible to Measure Happiness?' *European Journal for Philosophy of Science*, 3(2): 221–240.
Tiberius, V. and A. Plakias (2010). 'Well-Being' in J. Doris (ed.), *The Moral Psychology Handbook* (Oxford University Press).
Tiberius, V. and A. Hall (2010). 'Normative Theory and Psychological Research'. *The Journal of Positive Psychology*, 5(3): 212–225.

Happiness and other goods

Kauppinen, Antti (2013). 'Meaning and Happiness'. *Philosophical Topics*, 41(1): 161–185.

6 Hybrid theories of well-being

6.1 Introduction

So far we have examined a number of theories of well-being and found problems with each. To take just two examples, hedonism seemed problematic in failing to ascribe *any* prudential value to anything other than pleasure, a problem highlighted by the experience machine example.[1] By contrast, desire-fulfilment theory seemed to allow too *many* things to be good for us (because we have desires whose fulfilment plausibly does not connect with our own well-being).[2]

In this kind of situation, where we have a range of theories that each seem to be partly correct, but which face quite different objections, a natural question to ask is whether combining the theories in some way would yield an improvement over each considered alone. Can we combine the theories and thereby capture their virtues whilst avoiding the objections that threaten each? Theories that seek to do precisely this – 'hybrid theories' – are the subject of this chapter.

To understand the general idea of a hybrid theory it is worth seeing some examples. Take the following examples of hybrid theories (for simplicity I give only their claims about what is non-instrumentally good for us):

Pleasure and Desire hybrid theory

All and only desire-fulfilments that we take pleasure in are non-instrumentally good for us.

Pleasure and Achievement hybrid theory

All and only achievements that we take pleasure in are non-instrumentally good for us.

Perfections and Pleasure hybrid theory

All and only the exercise and development of our essential human capacities that we take pleasure in is good for us.[3]

(Henceforth I often omit the 'non-instrumentally', for the sake of readability. All claims about what is good for should be taken to be about what is non-instrumentally good for, unless otherwise specified.)

All three theories say that what is good for us is a certain *complex* thing. The first says that desire-fulfilment by itself is not what is good for us. Rather, it is desire-fulfilment *in which we take pleasure* that is good for us. The second says that achievement by itself is not what is good for us. Rather, it is achievement *in which we take pleasure* that is good for us. Finally, the third says that the exercise and development of essential human capacities by itself is not what is good for us. Rather, it is the exercise and development of these capacities *in which we take pleasure* that is good for us.

Hybrid theories vs pluralist theories

A natural question provoked by seeing these three example hybrid theories is: How, if at all, do hybrid theories differ from pluralist objective list theories, of the sort we saw in chapter 3?

The key difference is that pluralist objective lists specify a plurality of items that are *individually* good for us. By contrast, the hybrid theories above each specify a single, internally complex, item that is good for us. To see the difference let us compare the Pleasure and Achievement *hybrid* view:

Pleasure and Achievement hybrid theory

All and only achievements *that we take pleasure in* are non-instrumentally good for us.

against a *pluralist* view that says that pleasure and achievement are each well-being contributors:

Pleasure and Achievement pluralist theory

All achievements and all pleasures are non-instrumentally good for us.

We can represent the difference between these two views using the following convention of putting {} brackets around each well-being contributor specified by the theory:

Pleasure and Achievement hybrid theory

{Achievement in which pleasure is taken}

Pleasure and Achievement pluralist theory

{Achievement}, {Pleasure}

From this it is clear that the Pleasure and Achievement *pluralist* theory supplies two distinct well-being contributors.[4] Thus, according to the Pleasure and Achievement *pluralist* theory, achievement in which we take no pleasure *is* good for us and pleasure that is completely unrelated to achievement is good for us also.

By contrast, according to the Pleasure and Achievement *hybrid* theory what is good for us is only the combination of suitably related pleasure and achievement (so the pleasure must be pleasure *in* the achievement).

This contrast we have drawn between this particular hybrid theory and this particular pluralist objective list theory is one instance of the more general contrast between hybrid theories and pluralist objective list theories. The contrast is between theories that specify an internally complex prudential good and theories that specify a plurality of separate prudential goods.[5]

6.2 Can hybrid theories deliver the goods?

Can hybrid theories enjoy the best of both worlds when we combine the main elements of two theories? This is a difficult question to answer. After all, there are an *infinite* number of possible hybrid theories. For that reason it is impossible to assess hybrid theories *as such*. At best we can assess particular hybrid theories or groups of hybrid theories. I will focus first on this hybrid theory:

Hybrid theory 1: Pleasure and desire-fulfilment (P&D)

- All and only desire-fulfilments that we take pleasure in are non-instrumentally good for us.
- All and only desire frustrations that we take pain in are non-instrumentally bad for us.

(I will, however, only focus on the first half of the theory, due to constraints of space.)

Why focus on this particular hybrid theory? First, as a hybrid of two of the main theories of well-being, P&D is one that we can reasonably presume to be among the most promising possible hybrid theories. Second, hedonism and desire-fulfilment theory had quite *different* virtues and vices so examining a hybrid of these two theories will hopefully give some insight into the extent to which 'going hybrid' yields superior theories of well-being.

Before moving on to examine the theory in more detail, notice some questions that I am going to leave aside but which a hybrid theorist intending to defend P&D must address:

a How is the *overall* level of prudential value determined by the two elements, pleasure and desire-fulfilment? Is the degree of prudential value determined by both the intensity of the desire and the intensity of the pleasure or just one of these?[6]

b What does P&D say about the timing of the two elements? Must they be consecutive? Or can one element come later?[7] If I have a desire-fulfilment but only experience pleasure in it *much* later, does that satisfy P&D? Or must they be simultaneous (or at least very close).

c   Exactly what conditions must be fulfilled for the pleasure to be pleasure *in* the desire-fulfilment?

These are interesting questions of detail. But for now let us leave these questions aside. Instead, I will focus on these two guiding questions for investigating this Pleasure and Desire hybrid theory (P&D):

1   How does P&D compare with hedonism and desire-fulfilment theory?
2   What strengths and weaknesses does P&D have in its own right?

Let us start with the first question. In particular, what we should look to see is whether P&D has any major advantage or disadvantage as compared with hedonism and desire-fulfilment theory. Can it avoid objections faced by those theories?

6.3 How does P&D compare with hedonism and desire-fulfilment theory?

Avoiding problems with the experience machine?

Let us start with hedonism. As we saw in chapter 1, a major objection to hedonism is the experience machine objection. The example seems to undermine hedonism by giving cases where people at the same hedonic level do not seem necessarily to have the same level of well-being.

Here is an example we saw back in chapter 1

> **Trudy and Flora**: Trudy lives in New York. When not carrying on her ground-breaking research into stem cell treatment she enjoys running marathons, working for a local charity, skiing, socialising with friends and spending time with her life partner and their children. She also somehow finds time to pen highly successful, critically acclaimed, novels. She enjoys great physical health and springs out of bed every morning full of joy and excitement.
>
> Now meet Flora. When Flora was born she was attached to a machine that produces sensory stimulation and that gives her very rich, vivid, and life-like experiences. She has the pleasurable experience of carrying on ground-breaking research into stem cell treatment, of running marathons, of working for a local charity, skiing, socialising with friends and spending time with her life partner and their children. She also has the experience of writing highly successful and critically acclaimed novels. She is kept physically healthy by the machine and she also has the experience of springing out of bed every morning full of joy and excitement.

Let us make the plausible assumption that both Trudy and Flora desire to perform important research, run marathons, work for charity, have friends and a loving, etc. We can then summarise the case thus:

Table 6.1

	Hedonic Level	Desires	Desire-satisfied?
Trudy	+50	to do important research, run marathons, friends and family, etc.	Yes
Flora	+50	to do important research, run marathons, friends and family, etc.	No

What do P&D and hedonism say about Trudy and Flora?

Hedonism says that the non-hedonic features of Trudy and Flora's lives (whether they *actually* do things or merely have the experiences of doing them, whether their desires are satisfied, etc.) are irrelevant.[8] The fact that Trudy and Flora differ in these respects does not affect their well-being, according to hedonism. Hedonism ascribes equal prudential value to each pleasure and holds that nothing else determines their well-being. Their hedonic levels are the same so necessarily, according to hedonism, their levels of well-being are equal.

By contrast, P&D denies that Flora and Trudy have the same level of well-being. This is because, according to P&D, *only* Trudy's situation contains something with prudential value at all (because only her situation is one with a desire-fulfilment combined with pleasure in that desire-fulfilment). Whilst Flora experiences pleasure, her pleasure is not based on a desire-fulfilment but, rather, on the misleading experience of its being satisfied. Thus, according to P&D, there is *zero* prudential value in Flora's pleasure.[9]

What should we conclude from this? It will depend in large part on what we think that the experience machine shows. The judgement typically elicited by the experience machine example is that Flora and Trudy do not *necessarily* have equal levels of well-being and therefore hedonism is false (because it is committed to holding that they do). The key question is *why* that is true (on the assumption that it is). *Why* do Flora and Trudy have different levels of well-being? Here are two possible explanations:

Explanation 1: pleasures in the experience machine have *no* prudential value.

Explanation 2: a person's level of well-being is not solely determined by their hedonic level.[10]

As I argued in chapter 1, explanation 2 is preferable to explanation 1. It seems implausible that there is *no* prudential value in pleasures based on misleading experiences. For one thing, someone defending explanation 1 needs to supply a criterion for *how much* falsehood in one's beliefs about one's pleasurable experience deprives that pleasure of all prudential value. It seems that I can be a little mistaken about some aspects of my experience without this meaning that the pleasure I derive from it has zero prudential value. Suppose, for example, I am having the pleasurable experience of listening to you play the viola but I falsely believe you are playing a violin. Does that mistake rob my pleasurable experience of any prudential value? That seems implausible.

Another reason to doubt explanation 1 is that it seems implausible when transferred over to the case of pain. How bad for you some pain is seems to depend on its felt qualities. It does not seem to be affected by whether the beliefs that prompt it are true or false. If that is so then that is evidence that explanation 1 is implausible in the case of pleasure (assuming that pleasure and pain are symmetrical in this respect). Without providing a comprehensive argument for it here, I suggest that explanation 2 offers the better explanation of experience machine cases.

Here is how the choice between explanations 1 and 2 impacts upon our assessment of P&D. If one accepts explanation 1 – and holds that pleasures in experience machine cases have zero prudential value – one might then conclude that P&D enjoys an advantage over hedonism in experience machine cases. This would be on the grounds that according to P&D, Flora's life has no positive well-being contributors (because she doesn't have any pleasure derived from desire-fulfilment).

However, if, as I have suggested, explanation 1 is problematic then we should conclude that P&D is actually *more* vulnerable to the experience machine objection, and objections of its general type, than hedonism is. Hedonism is vulnerable to the experience machine example in being forced to hold that Flora and Trudy have *equal* levels of well-being. But whilst P&D generates the plausible comparative claim that Trudy is better off, it secures this result at a significant cost. That significant cost is having to hold that Flora's pleasure has *zero* prudential value (because it is not based on a desire-fulfilment). But that seems implausible. From this we should conclude that P&D is *more* vulnerable to the experience machine than hedonism is and thus incurs a significant *disadvantage* as compared with hedonism.

Problematic pleasures/desire-fulfilments

Another kind of objection is one that applies both to hedonism and to desire-fulfilment theories. The objection alleges that these theories ascribe prudential value to problematic things. Applied to hedonism the objection targets the claim that *all* pleasures have prudential value. The corresponding objection for desire-fulfilment theory targets the claim that all desire-fulfilments have prudential value.

One particular example that is typically used in pushing this kind of objection to these theories is the example of *malicious* pleasures and desire-fulfilments. Consider this case:

> **Malicious Melisandre 1**: Melisandre experiences pleasure when seeing people and animals in pain.

Malicious Melisandre 2: Melisandre desires that people and animals be in pain, desires that regularly get fulfilled.[11]

To the extent that these cases are a problem for hedonism and desire-fulfilment theory, does P&D fare better? It seems not. The trouble for hedonism in cases of malicious pleasure is that Melisandre 1 takes pleasure in something horrible, such as suffering, and hedonism must say that such pleasures are prudentially valuable. The problem thus had nothing to do with Melisandre 1's desires not being fulfilled. So P&D's addition – the requirement that the pleasure is based on a desire-fulfilment (the desire for the suffering of others, presumably) – is no sort of remedy to the original problem.

We get the same result with desire-fulfilment theory. The original problem for desire-fulfilment views is their ascribing prudential value to the fulfilment of desires for problematic things, such as in Melisandre 2. If this is a problem, it seems no solution to require that the desire-fulfilments must also be enjoyed. The worry for desire-fulfilment theory from problematic desires is not that it seems problematic to allow such desire-fulfilments to have prudential value, even when not enjoyed. The problem is that of ascribing prudential value to these problematic desire-fulfilments *at all*.

In the vast majority of cases of an agent who engages in problematic enjoyment of someone's suffering there will be an overlap between (a) taking pleasure in something (some person's suffering) and (b) a desire being fulfilled. After all, presumably most people who enjoy the suffering of others desire it in advance and most people who desire the suffering of others take enjoyment from its occurring. Thus desire-fulfilment theory, hedonism, and P&D will overlap in their answers about most cases of problematic pleasure/desire-fulfilment. The only cases where they will give different verdicts are:

i   problematic pleasure without desire-fulfilment
ii   problematic desire-fulfilment without pleasure.

Hedonism ascribes prudential value to (i). Desire-fulfilment theory ascribes prudential value to (ii). P&D, by contrast, will ascribe prudential value to neither (i) nor (ii). From this we might be tempted to conclude that P&D enjoys a major advantage over hedonism and desire-fulfilment theory with respect to problematic pleasure/desire. However, on closer examination, we see that this is a mistake for two reasons.

First, P&D gives the wrong answer in the most typical case, the case where the malicious pleasure and desire-fulfilment are both present (it says of such cases that these combinations are prudentially valuable).

Second, and more importantly, P&D gives the wrong explanation of *why* there is nothing prudentially valuable about (i) and (ii). P&D must say that (ii) is not prudentially valuable *because* this problematic desire-fulfilment is unaccompanied by pleasure. And P&D must say that (i) is not prudentially valuable because this malicious pleasure is not accompanied by desire-fulfilment. P&D must say of each case that if the missing ingredient were present there *would* be something prudentially valuable. To the extent that one thinks that problematic pleasure or desire-fulfilment does not have prudential value, I take it that one is unlikely to think that adding the other element *improves* things. Thus P&D does not enjoy an advantage over hedonism and desire-fulfilment when it comes to problematic pleasures and desire. To the extent that one thinks that the original objection from malicious pleasures or desires is a problem for desire-fulfilment theory and hedonism, one should think that P&D is no improvement. It faces this objection just as much as the other two theories do.[12]

The scope problem

The main objection to desire-fulfilment theory was the scope problem.[13] We first saw the scope problem in connection with examples such as these:

> **The Stranger on a Plane**: On a plane from London to Madrid, Lucy meets Ben who tells her that he's going to a remote village in Spain to marry his childhood sweetheart, John. Lucy leaves the plane desiring that Ben is successful in this and that he lives a happy life. This happens but Lucy never hears from them and never travels near there again (nor do they ever visit England).

> **Life on Mars**: In 2014, Hilary desires that there is life elsewhere in the universe. Unbeknownst to all humans (and only discovered after her death) there is life on Mars in 2014.

The problem for desire-fulfilment theory is that it holds that these desire-fulfilments have prudential value when, intuitively, they seem not to. (Keep in mind that they never learn of the desire-fulfilments.)

Does P&D fare better when it comes to these kinds of cases? Let us remember the stipulation that in these cases, Lucy and Hilary experience no pleasure in connection with these desires – on account of their never coming to believe that their desire has been fulfilled.[14] The main details of the cases are thus:

Table 6.2

	Desires	Desire satisfied?	Pleasure in desire-fulfilment?
Lucy	happy marriage for Ben and John	Yes	0
Hilary	life elsewhere in the universe	Yes	0

According to desire-fulfilment theory there *is* prudential value in each situation because there is a desire-fulfilment in each (the absence of pleasure is irrelevant). This result is the basis for the scope problem.

P&D will give the result that there is *no* prudential value in this situation. P&D says that for there to be prudential value it would have to be the case that Hilary and Lucy took pleasure in the desire-fulfilment. That is, we would need to add pleasure to the desire-fulfilment (and this pleasure would need to be pleasure in the desire-fulfilment).

Compare the cases of Lucy and Hilary as described above with alternate cases, cases where they take pleasure in the fulfilment of their desires. In these alternate cases, it seems more plausible that there *is* prudential value. If Lucy desires that Ben and John are happy and, knowing that they are, takes pleasure in this, that certainly seems to be more plausibly good for Lucy. Thus P&D seems to give the right answer in the original scope problem case (where the desire is fulfilled without any awareness or pleasure in this) and in the alternate case (where the desire is fulfilled and there is awareness and resulting pleasure). For that reason it looks like P&D has an advantage over the desire-fulfilment theory view in avoiding the scope problem.

Let us summarise what we have seen so far. We have looked at three objections invoked against hedonism and desire-fulfilment theory:

1   the experience machine objection (which applies to hedonism)
2   the problem of problematic pleasure/desire-fulfilments (which applies to both theories)
3   the scope problem (which applies to desire-fulfilment theory).

Our main question has been whether P&D is any more or less vulnerable to these objections than hedonism and desire-fulfilment theory. Our answers have been mixed. P&D seems *more* vulnerable than hedonism to the experience machine objection. It seems *equally* vulnerable to the objection from problematic pleasures/desire-fulfilments. By contrast, P&D seems *less* vulnerable than desire-fulfilment theory with respect to the scope problem.

From this it seems that we should conclude that *when it comes to these objections* P&D is less plausible than hedonism but more plausible than desire-fulfilment theory.

Let us move on now to our *second* guiding question by examining P&D in its own right. I will begin by explaining a pair of objections to P&D. The first targets the desire-fulfilment aspect of P&D, arguing that this is too strong. The second targets the pleasure requirement of P&D, arguing that this is too strong.

6.4 Second guiding question: how does P&D fare in its own right?

Objection 1: desire-fulfilment is not necessary for prudential value

In discussing how P&D fares with respect to the scope problem we introduced variants on the original Lucy and Hilary cases. In the variant cases, Lucy and Hilary's desires are fulfilled *and* they take pleasure in the fulfilment of their desires.

Thinking about these cases provokes the question of whether the desire-fulfilment requirement helps or hinders P&D. To see the issue, let us compare *three* cases (to keep things simple I will consider three versions of the Lucy case but the same points apply to the Hilary case). One is the original Lucy case, the second is the variant we considered above, the third is a new variant (one where Lucy's desire is not fulfilled but, *believing* that it is fulfilled, she experiences pleasure):

Table 6.3

	Desires	Desire-fulfilled?	Believes desire to be fulfilled?	Hedonic level
Lucy	happy marriage for Ben and John	Yes	No	0
Lucy 2	happy marriage for Ben and John	Yes	Yes	+25
Lucy 3	happy marriage for Ben and John	No	Yes	+25

What does P&D say about these cases? P&D says there is prudential value in case 2 only. For only in this case do we have the combination of both desire-fulfilment and pleasure in that desire-fulfilment. P&D says that there is no prudential value in case 1 (because there is no pleasure) and no prudential value in case 3 (because there is no desire-fulfilment). Whilst Lucy believes that her desire is fulfilled, and is pleased, her desire is not in fact fulfilled. Thus according to P&D there is no prudential value.

Looking at cases 2 and 3, one might wonder whether this requirement of desire-fulfilment is a good feature of P&D. After all, one might wonder whether we should treat cases 2 and 3 *so* differently, such that there is prudential value in case 2 but *none* in case 3. One might wonder whether the requirement that the pleasure be based on the real fulfilment of a desire is too strong. After all, one might argue, is there really *no* prudential value in case 3, a case of (mistakenly) believing that your desire is fulfilled, and taking great pleasure in that? Is there not even a little prudential value in this?

What this case of Lucy 3 (and the experience machine example of Flora discussed above) bring out is that the desire-*fulfilment* requirement of P&D might be too strong and thereby weaken the theory overall. There are at least some cases where it seems that there is some prudential value even though there is no desire-fulfilment. To the extent that one is sympathetic to this objection, one will think that P&D has at least one problematic feature (one that it inherits from the desire-fulfilment theory view).

The objection to P&D that we have just considered pointed out that there are cases – such as Lucy 3 (and Flora) – where it is plausible that there is prudential value even though there is no fulfilment of the agent's desires. If this is right then P&D makes a mistake in claiming that all prudential value has desire-fulfilment as a necessary element.

One might push this kind of objection further, by arguing that just as desire-*fulfilment* is not always necessary for prudential value, neither is *desire* itself. That is, one might argue that there are cases of prudential value without any relevant desire.[15] If this were true then P&D would be false, given that it claims that *all* prudential value is comprised of desire-fulfilments in which the agent takes pleasure. The important question is whether it is plausible that there are cases of prudential value without desire.

One such example is the following:

> **Miserable Maud**. Maud is a fully committed ascetic who thinks that all pleasure is the devil's work and forbidden by her deity. Unbeknownst to Maud she has extremely pleasurable dreams on a nightly basis, dreams that she does not recall upon waking.

Plausibly this pleasure is good for Maud. If that is right then there is prudential value without desire (let alone desire-fulfilment). Another such example comes from developing self-respect:

> **Sally's Self-Respect**: Sally's upbringing left her with a low sense of self-worth and self-respect. However, after a difficult youth, she is successful in her career and in love. Her career success, coupled with finding love, lead her to gradually develop self-respect. However, at no point prior to acquiring this self-respect did she desire it. She never gave it much thought and, if she had considered the issue, she wouldn't have recognised that she *lacked* self-respect and so wouldn't have desired to acquire it.

Plausibly it was good for Sally to develop self-respect. If that is right then there is prudential value without desire (let alone desire-fulfilment).[16]

These are just two possible cases. But if either of them (or some other case of their general form) is possible then there are cases where something has prudential value for a person without the person desiring that thing (and thus without its *fulfilling* a desire of theirs). But this is a possibility that P&D must deny. If P&D is true then these cases are not possible (nor can there be any other cases of their general form). For according to P&D all instances of prudential value are composed of desire-fulfilment and pleasure in that desire-fulfilment. To the extent that we think that the cases feature something of prudential value then we should think that P&D is mistaken to hold that all prudential value is partly a matter of desire-fulfilment.

Objection 2: Pleasure is not necessary for prudential value

Having considered the objection that P&D goes wrong in holding that desire-fulfilment is a necessary constituent of all prudential value, we should now examine a different objection. This objection is that P&D goes wrong in holding that *pleasure* is an essential ingredient of all prudential value.

One very general way of objecting to P&D on these grounds would be to point out that if there can be people incapable of experiencing pleasure (something that certainly seems plausible, and plausibly actual) then P&D is committed to the claim that there are *no* prudential goods for these people, no matter what their lives are like. And one might think that that is too strong, that there could be *some* things that are good for people even if they are unable to experience pleasure.

Moving away from the general possibility of people who cannot experience pleasure, one might argue that there are plausible cases of prudential value where a person happens not to experience pleasure. Here is one such example.

> **Rae's Recital**: Rae is a classical musician who will be performing at a highly distinguished venue. Her perfectionist tendencies mean that she practises continually for months with meticulous care and attention. She desperately desires to give a perfect performance. On the day it goes flawlessly; her performance is magnificent. However, she does not experience any pleasure in connection with the performance. Her pre-performance nerves rob her of any enjoyment in the build up. And during the performance her focus is entirely on getting the music right. Then, after the performance she remains so unconvinced that it went well that she takes no pleasure from it.

It seems plausible that Rae's successful recital is good for her. (Leave aside the question of exactly *why* this is so. Perhaps it is because giving a brilliant recital satisfies one of her desires or perhaps because it is simply a wonderful achievement.) But given that there is no pleasure in the fulfilment of the desire – because of the missing pleasure – P&D must deny that the successful recital was good for Rae *at all*.[17] Many will find this counterintuitive. They might argue as follows: whilst it would be *better* for Rae if she took pleasure in her brilliant performance that does not mean that there was *nothing* good for her in the actual case (where she does not take pleasure in it). Cases like Rae's perhaps show that P&D is too demanding in requiring that pleasure be a necessary element in *every* instance of prudential value.

Interim summary

What have we seen so far? We started off examining the prospects for P&D as compared with hedonism and desire-fulfilment theory. We did this by looking at how P&D fares against some stock objections to each theory. P&D was inferior to hedonism but it enjoyed an advantage over DFT (in avoiding the scope problem).

In this latest section we have examined the merits of P&D in its own right, by asking whether it generates plausible answers. We have seen two main objections to the view. The first is that P&D is mistaken in holding that desire-fulfilment is an essential feature of all cases of prudential value. The second is that P&D is mistaken in holding that pleasure is an essential feature of all cases of prudential value. We looked at a range of cases designed to support these objections. Some are cases of prudential value without desire-fulfilment (Lucy 3, Maud, Sally). Others are cases of prudential value without pleasure (Rae).

Thinking once more about *comparative* plausibility, notice that P&D is in a worse position than hedonism and desire-fulfilment theory. Both hedonism and DFT are subject to one of these objections. But P&D must fend off *both* objections. So even if the objection based on desire-fulfilment can be fended off by P&D, there is still the objection based on pleasure. By contrast, each of hedonism and desire-fulfilment theory is vulnerable to only one of these objections.[18]

From the arguments and objections that we have considered so far it seems that P&D enjoys *no* advantage over hedonism and desire-fulfilment theory. With one exception (the scope problem) P&D inherits each objection to which either hedonism or desire-fulfilment theory is vulnerable. Thus rather than being a way of attracting the merits of each theory and share the spoils available to each, it seems to combine the *worst* of the two theories and be vulnerable to (nearly) every problem faced by the other theory. This is defeasible evidence that the idea of 'going hybrid' in order to develop more plausible theories of well-being might not be so promising.[19] In the rest of the chapter I will examine a second hybrid theory to see if we get the same results – that the hybrid theory does not improve upon the non-hybrid equivalent theory.

6.5 A second hybrid theory

Our first hybrid theory, P&D, we examined in some detail before determining that it offers no advantage over the pure theories that it was a hybrid of (namely desire-fulfilment theory and hedonism). Let us now look at a second hybrid theory in order to continue accumulating data about the prospects for hybrid theories in general.

When we examined objective list theories we found that a common objection to such theories is that they are implausibly alienating, in virtue of allowing things to be good for someone who does not desire or care about those things. A natural suggestion, then, is to see whether we can come up with a better theory if we 'hybridise' an objective list theory. Thus let us consider a hybrid theory formed by taking a regular, pluralist, objective list theory and 'hybridising' it through adding a desire element.

In examining objective list theories we considered this theory, which I called 'three goods':

Three goods objective list theory

All and only pleasure, friendship, and achievement have prudential value

Let us now construct a hybrid theory thus:

Three goods hybrid theory [TGHT]

Three things have prudential value: (i) Pleasure that is desired (ii) Friendship that is desired (iii) Achievement that is desired.

Following the convention of using {} to denote well-being contributors we can represent these theories thus:

Three goods objective list theory

{pleasure}, {friendship}, {achievement}

Three goods hybrid theory

{pleasure that is desired}, {friendship that is desired}, {achievement that is desired}

Unlike P&D, which was monistic, this hybrid theory – TGHT – is *pluralistic*. It says that there is more than one thing with prudential value. But it also says that *each* prudential good is an internally complex combination of something and desire.

What I propose to do now is to examine the extent to which TGHT can overcome the difficulties faced by our previous hybrid theory (P&D), to see if it is a superior hybrid theory. We will then ask whether it is generally a good theory of well-being.

6.6 Does TGHT fare any better than P&D?

To answer this question, remember how the other theories fared against the problem cases:[20]

Table 6.4

	Hedonism	*Desire-fulfilment theory*	*P&D*
Experience machine [Trudy and Flora]	objection	no objection	objection
Malicious pleasure/desire [Melisandre]	objection	objection	objection
Scope problem [Lucy, Hilary]	no objection	objection	no objection
Pleasure without desire-fulfilment [Lucy 3, Flora]	no objection	objection	objection
Pleasure without desire [Maud]	no objection	objection	objection
Self-respect without desire [Sally]	objection	objection	objection
Desire-fulfilling achievement with no pleasure [Rae]	objection	no objection	objection

Here is a reminder of the tenets of TGHT:

Three Goods Hybrid Theory [TGHT]

Three things have prudential value: (i) Pleasure that is desired (ii) Friendship that is desired (iii) Achievement that is desired.

Let us see how TGHT fares across this set of cases.[21]

Experience machine

Suppose we think, as I have urged, that two things are true of the experience machine example: (1) Trudy's well-being is higher than Flora's (2) Flora's false pleasures have some prudential value. Can TGHT deliver this result? Certainly there is no friendship or achievement for Flora in the experience machine whereas there is (desired) friendship and achievement for Trudy. So TGHT certainly supports (1). Whether TGHT supports (2) depends on what exactly Flora's desires are. But let us suppose that Trudy and Flora only desire pleasure that is connected to friendship and achievement. That is, neither desires the kind of experience machine pleasure that Flora experiences (suppose that Flora would be horrified to discover that she was in the experience machine).[22] On that assumption, TGHT faces a problem with the experience machine case. Because the pleasures that Flora experiences are not desired by Flora, TGHT must say that they have zero prudential value. Thus, it would seem that, like P&D, TGHT is vulnerable to the experience machine objection.

Malicious pleasure/desire

TGHT will be just as vulnerable as P&D to the objection from malicious pleasure. Both theories give the problematic result that Melisandre's malicious pleasures are good for her in the typical case where the pleasures are desired. And they both say the wrong thing about malicious pleasures that are not desired (namely that the addition of a desire for them would mean that such pleasures have prudential value). Thus this objection applies equally to TGHT as to P&D.

The scope problem

TGHT does not hold that mere desire-fulfilment alone has prudential value. So TGHT does not give the problematic result in the case of Lucy and Hilary that the fulfilment of their desires is good for them. It is thus, like P&D, not vulnerable to the scope problem.

Pleasure without desire-fulfilment

Lucy 3 (like Flora) plausibly does not desire the pleasure that she experiences (a pleasure based on the false belief that her desire is fulfilled). Thus TGHT must say that her pleasure has no prudential value. In that way, TGHT is just as vulnerable as P&D to objections based on cases like Lucy 3 (and Flora), cases of pleasure without desire-fulfilment.

Pleasure without desire

Miserable Maud experiences pleasure that she certainly does not desire. TGHT must therefore say that her pleasurable dreams have no prudential value. Thus TGHT is equally as vulnerable as P&D to objections based on cases of pleasure without desire.

Self-respect without desire

TGHT must say that Sally's developing self-respect is not good for her. After all, Sally does not desire to develop self-respect (remember that she gives it no thought and, if she did, she would falsely believe that she already has self-respect) nor is it clearly one of the three goods on the list. Thus TGHT is just as vulnerable as P&D to objections based on cases of self-respect without desire.[23]

Desire-fulfilling achievement with no pleasure

Rae's achievement is an achievement that she desires but takes no pleasure in. Unlike P&D, TGHT can say that it has prudential value for her even without any pleasure being taken in it. Thus, unlike P&D, TGHT is not vulnerable to cases of desire-fulfilling achievement that nonetheless does not generate pleasure.

From this, we see that TGHT is plausibly vulnerable to *fewer* of these objections than P&D is. It thus seems the superior of the two hybrid theories

Table 6.5

	P&D	TGHT
Experience machine [Trudy and Flora]	objection	objection
Malicious pleasure/desire [Melisandre]	objection	objection
Scope problem [Lucy, Hilary]	no objection	no objection
Pleasure without desire-fulfilment [Lucy 3, Flora]	objection	objection
Pleasure without desire [Maud]	objection	objection
Self-respect without desire [Sally]	objection	objection
Desire-fulfilling achievement with no pleasure [Rae]	objection	no objection

we have considered here. Note, however, that that is only to make *one* of the two important comparisons we need to make, as part of our inquiry into whether hybrid theories offer better prospects for theorising about well-being than non-hybrid theories. When we assessed P&D we compared it with the *non*-hybrid theories that it was built up from (hedonism and desire-fulfilment theory). Thus we should, in a similar fashion, compare TGHT with its non-hybrid equivalent (the three goods objective list theory).

6.7 Does TGHT fare any better than its non-hybrid equivalent?

TGHT was developed by taking the three good objective list theory and adding a desire-fulfilment requirement. So how does TGHT compare with the theory upon which it was based?

Like TGHT, the three goods objective list theory upon which it is based is vulnerable to the objection from malicious pleasures. It thus shares one kind of vulnerability. However, it is plausible that the three goods objective list theory gives more plausible answers in *all* of the cases where TGHT goes awry. This is because it is precisely the additional desire element that makes TGHT vulnerable to the other objections. TGHT's claim that pleasure, achievement and friendship are only prudentially valuable *when desired* is the source of the objections it faces in the case of Flora, Lucy 3, and Maud (each of whom experiences pleasure that they do not desire). Without that element, the three goods objective list theory can say that there is prudential value to the pleasures in these cases, irrespective of whether they are desired. It can thus give the result that the pleasures of Flora, Lucy 3 and Maud have prudential value.

The three goods objective list theory *may* also be able to avoid the objection based on the case of Sally (that of someone developing self-respect that they do not desire to develop). Here is how. Suppose, plausibly, that developing self-respect is an achievement. Even if this is not an achievement that she desires, it is nonetheless an achievement. If it is an achievement, though one that she does not desire, then the three goods objective list theory (unlike TGHT) can still attribute prudential value to it simply on the basis of its being an achievement.

The upshot of this is twofold. TGHT is the better of the two *hybrid* theories considered in this chapter – at least when it comes to these objections. But with respect to these objections what makes it a hybrid theory (its incorporation of a desire element) brings about no improvement over the non-hybrid equivalent theory, the three goods objective list theory.[24]

What should we conclude from this? Once again, it seems that we should conclude that, to the extent that the problem cases identified above are problem cases, 'going hybrid' offers no significant advantage in developing a theory of well-being. P&D was vulnerable to *more* objections than the non-hybrid theories upon which it was based. The same is true of TGHT. In the latter case the non-hybrid theory seems *much* less vulnerable to these objections.[25] From this, it seems that the prospects for going hybrid might not be very positive. At the same time, though, we must be cautious as we have only considered two hybrid theories and there are other possible theories.

6.8 Conclusion

In this chapter we have examined hybrid theories of well-being, theories that try in some way to marry two existing theories of well-being and plunder the spoils available to each. One point we noted at the beginning of the chapter is that there are an infinite number of such theories, which makes it difficult to provide an assessment of the hybrid route in general. To make partial progress, we examined two theories, one that combined hedonism and desire-fulfilment theory (P&D) and another that hybridised an objective list theory by adding a desire element (TGHT).

The first theory we considered (P&D) yielded a theory that, though an improvement on desire-fulfilment theory, was not clearly any better than hedonism. The second theory we considered (TGHT) was the better of the two hybrid theories we examined. Nevertheless, this theory was actually more vulnerable to objections than the non-hybridised objective list theory upon which it was based.

Of course there are limitations to the case against hybrid theories built here. First, we have only considered two hybrid theories. Second, we have assumed that these objections are good objections, which one might very well dispute (I have also tended to implicitly assume that the objections are equally serious, which one could certainly dispute). Third, we have only examined *some* of the potential objections that might be levelled against each of these hybrid theories. It is not possible to definitively conclude anything about hybrid theories in general from the considerations of this chapter. But what we have seen in this chapter *suggests* that 'going hybrid' is not going to straightforwardly improve our chances of finding the correct theory of well-being.

Comprehension questions

1   Why does P&D avoid the experience machine objection?
2   Why does P&D fare equally well (badly) as hedonism/desire-fulfilment theory with the objection based on malicious pleasures/desires?
3   How does TGHT differ from the three goods objective list theory?

Further questions

1   How does the pleasure and desire-fulfilment hybrid theory (P&D) compare with a pluralist view, one on which both pleasure and desire-fulfilment

has prudential value? What does this view say about the problem cases we have examined? Does it do better or worse overall?

2   In the cases of Flora and Lucy 3, what difference would it make to the answers given by DFT, P&D, TGHT, if we assumed that they each have a desire for pleasure per se/in general?

3   Does TGHT have any advantages over the three goods objective list theory? Can it avoid any objections to that theory?

4   In this chapter I focused on the positive side of P&D (its claim about what is good for us). Is the negative side of P&D more or less plausible than the positive side?

Notes

1   See chapter 1.
2   See chapter 2.
3   This theory is in some ways similar to the developmentalism defended by Kraut (2007). For other hybrid theories see Adams (1999) and Kagan (2009).
4   They are distinct even if they overlap on some occasions, such as when someone takes pleasure in some achievement.
5   The qualitative hedonism that was mentioned in chapter 1 – the idea that pleasures have different qualities which determine their prudential value – is another kind of hybrid view.
6   You might wonder what other answers are possible. Here is one: a desire and pleasure must each be present but the degree of intensity of desire is not relevant to the overall prudential value whereas increases in the degree of pleasure always increase the overall prudential value. For discussion of these issues see Sarch (2012), Woodard (2016).
7   Suppose I am in a coma when the desire-fulfilment occurs and am not conscious until quite some time later. For more discussion of these issues, see Kagan (2009).
8   More precisely, such non-hedonic features are only instrumentally relevant, relevant because of what their hedonic effects might be.
9   Keep in mind that Flora's desire is to *actually* run marathons (etc.), not merely to have the experience of what it would be like.
10   Notice that explanation 2 is consistent with pleasures in the experience machine having some prudential value.
11   Melisandre 1 is the form of the objection that hedonism is vulnerable to. Melisandre 2 is the form of the objection that desire-fulfilment theory is vulnerable to.
12   Someone sympathetic to the P&D theory, like some hedonists, might try to avoid this problem by making the theory a little more complicated by introducing a qualitative element, by allowing for different qualities of pleasure and desire-fulfilment. I lack the space to explore such a possibility here. Would such a theory be an improvement over P&D? Would it face any new problems?
13   One could think of the previous objection as just a further instance of this general objection.
14   They might experience pleasure in other things but that would not be relevant, according to P&D.
15   For discussion of this kind of objection, see Lauinger (2013), Sarch (2012).
16   Note that in this case there is also no pleasure in the fulfilment of a desire either.
17   If you find it difficult to imagine Rae taking no pleasure – even a long time later – you can add the supposition that she dies soon after the performance (without losing the sense that it did not go so well).
18   Remember that hedonists can allow cases of prudential value without desire and desire-fulfilment theorists can allow for cases of prudential value without pleasure.
19   Of course, this is only one instance of a hybrid theory so it is not decisive evidence.

20 To be clear, I am *not* assuming that the objections definitely cannot be answered, only that there is a prima facie case against the theory, based on the cases. Nor am I assuming that this is a *definitive* list of objections.
21 I do not describe the cases in detail again here.
22 If you find this case weird, think about cases like the experience machine but which just rely on ignorance or deception, rather than peculiar technology. I take it that when we think of such cases we can imagine not desiring to experience these kinds of pleasures, pleasures based on illusion or deception.
23 Possible objection: Sally's developing self-respect is an achievement and so good for her for that reason. Reply: it is *not* an achievement *that Sally desires*. So TGHT still must say that it fails to be good for her, given that it is not an achievement that she desires.
24 One alternative to TGHT perhaps worth exploring is one that drops the requirement that plea-sure be desired in order to be prudentially valuable, whilst retaining the desire requirement on achievement and friendship.
25 Again, I have not considered all possible objections to either theory. So I am not claiming that TGHT is definitely the weaker, only that is seems weaker based on consideration of these cases. And I have not discussed things that each theory might have in their favour. One thing that TGHT might have in its favour, some may claim, is a reduced vulnerability to the alienation objection. That might be so but I lack the space to discuss it here. See the 'further questions' for more on this.

References

Adams, Robert M. (1999). *Finite and Infinite Goods. A Framework for Ethics* (Oxford University Press).

Kagan, Shelly (2009). 'Well-Being as Enjoying the Good'. *Philosophical Perspectives*, 23(1): 253–272.

Kraut, Richard (2007). *What is Good and Why: The Ethics of Well-Being* (Harvard University Press).

Lauinger, William (2013). 'The Missing-Desires Objection to Hybrid Theories of Well-Being'. *The Southern Journal of Philosophy*, 51(2): 270–295.

Sarch, Alex F. (2012). 'Multi-Component Theories of Well-Being and Their Structure'. *Pacific Philosophical Quarterly*, 93(4): 439–471.

Woodard, Christopher (2016). 'Hybrid Theories' in G. Fletcher (ed.), *Routledge Handbook of Philosophy of Well-Being* (Routledge).

7   Well-being and the shape of a life

7.1 Introduction

In the previous chapters we examined theories of well-being, theories of which things have prudential value and why. These theories were implicitly focused on the kinds of prudential goods and bads that someone might have at a point in time (pleasure, pain, friendship) and so helped us to think about the question of how well someone is doing at some point in their life. A distinct question that we have so far neglected is how the well-being or prudential value of *a whole life* is determined. In this chapter we turn to that question. In particular we will examine a recent claim that a person's lifetime well-being is not straightforwardly determined by their level of well-being at each point in their life (something called the 'shape of a life hypothesis', to be further explained shortly). We will begin by looking at what the phenomenon is supposed to be. We will then examine various arguments that attempt to debunk or explain away the phenomenon. Finally we will ask what it would mean if the shape of a life phenomenon is genuine.

7.2 The shape of a life hypothesis introduced

Before looking at an explicit formulation of the shape of a life hypothesis, let us begin with this pair of cases:

> **Uppi's life and Downey's life:** Uppi and Downey are twins whose parents are tragically killed within hours of their birth and who are then separated and raised completely separately. Their lives take very different courses.
> *Early years (0–20)* Uppi is raised in poverty and has severe health problems that are exacerbated by having to work full time cleaning factories to support herself. She has no free time, few material goods, little formal education, and no time for friendships or play. She is miserable and exhausted almost every day.
> Downey is raised by an affluent loving family who live within a close-knit community. She enjoys excellent education, she makes many firm friends, she excels at sport and science regularly winning junior olympiads and representing her country at football. She is cheerful and happy almost every day.

Middle Years (20–47) Uppi spends most of her 20s, 30s and 40s working in the factory. The work is still hard and the hours long but eventually stricter government regulations coupled with technological development means that the work gradually becomes less laborious. Her health gradually improves as a result of moving from manual work to operating a computer. Her wages increase as a result of equality legislation, enabling her to move to a less polluted area. She is finally able to enjoy life, bit by bit. She makes friends at the factory and in her local community. Each year goes a little better than the previous one.

Downey goes to college at a prestigious American university. During her final semester she attends a party and meets George. Hitting it off with him immediately, they decide to drive to a nearby bar. On the way they are involved in a car accident in which a child is killed. She is found not guilty of causing death by dangerous driving but, as the driver, Downey is racked by guilt. She attempts to return to university and despite making some progress on her course, she is shunned by her peers in light of the accident. Her grades suffer, she is a depressed recluse but eventually she graduates with a mediocre degree. After college, she becomes a call-centre worker. She hates her job, lives at home with her parents, has no social life or interests and, though constantly haunted by the feeling that her early promise has been wasted, is unable to stick to any plan to get her life back on track. Each year is worse than the previous one. Eventually she has no self-confidence or sense that her life could be any better.

Last Section (47–70) Aged 47, Uppi literally bumps into one of the suppliers to the factory. To apologise for knocking her over, the factory supplier offers to buy her dinner. She accepts. They get on very well and become good friends. Learning of her life and near-poverty, the supplier is moved to help Uppi. She gives her money to sort out her remaining health problems, and sufficient money to enable her to work part-time and to enrol in night classes in engineering. Uppi turns out to be naturally adept at engineering and is offered a full scholarship to a prestigious American university. There she excels at engineering, graduating *magna cum laude* and develops a number of rewarding hobbies and interests. She is also extremely popular, making many firm friendships and falling in love with a fellow mature student. After college, Uppi and her partner work for a charity that develops and distributes cheap, secure, housing to developing countries. They live in a welcoming secure neighbourhood and enjoy many hobbies and interests with their friends. Uppi's work is internationally recognised and she is invited to join many international organisations to advise on how to alleviate poverty and improve housing in developing countries. She is sufficiently affluent to have zero money worries. Upon hearing of her remarkable life-story she is persuaded by publishers to write an autobiography, which is well-received. She loves her job and is able to continue in advisory roles after her retirement (she is not the sort of person who could simply retire) before dying peacefully in her sleep at 70.

Aged 47, Downey's well-meaning parents send her to a rehab clinic at an exotic location to try to break the cycle that she is in. There, finally, she reaches resolution over the accident and decides that, upon returning home, she will re-enrol in university and try to get her life on track. Unfortunately, when Downey is at the airport returning home from her exotic rehab clinic she is targeted by a drug trafficker who, unbeknownst to her, puts liquid cocaine in her luggage. This is detected and Downey is arrested. Deprived access to proper legal advice, Downey is forced to sign a confession under the false pretence of its being a contract to pay a small fine for her release. She is denied bail and is continually prevented from obtaining adequate legal representation. Eventually her trial is heard and she is found guilty of drug trafficking. Her sentence is 25 years. She spends the rest of her days in a squalid jail cell working in the prison kitchen for the pittance that she spends on prison-acquired addictions. She is miserable and exhausted almost every day and finally dies of an overdose at 70.

Uppi and Downey are only particular examples.[1] Their significance, for now, is that they demonstrate the possibility of lives that go 'uphill' and 'downhill' respectively. It is very plausible that Uppi's life initially has a low level of well-being before things steadily improve, before improving a lot in the last section of life. By contrast, Downey initially has a high level of well-being before things steadily decline and then declining a lot in the last section of life.[2]

It will be useful now to distinguish two different things that we might be interested in:

Momentary well-being: a person's level of well-being/how well things are going for that person at a time T1 or between two times T2 – T3.

Lifetime well-being: a person's overall lifetime well-being/how well the person's whole life goes.

To see the difference, notice the difference between the question of how well Uppi's *life* went from the question of how well her *childhood* went, or how her well-being was when she was 18. When I talk about Uppi and Downey's lives going 'uphill'/'downhill' I mean that their *momentary* well-being continues to increase/decrease as the life progresses. By contrast, a person's *lifetime* well-being is an evaluation of the well-being of their life as a whole. It is plausibly only settled once a person's life has finished.

We now have the distinction between momentary and lifetime well-being in hand.[3] Here are two claims that one might hold about the *relation* between momentary and lifetime well-being:

Additivism about lifetime well-being: A person's lifetime well-being is fully determined by their total amount of momentary well-being. Any two lives with the same *sum* of momentary well-being necessarily have the same lifetime well-being (and vice versa).

Holism about lifetime well-being: A person's *lifetime* well-being is not fully determined by their total amount of *momentary* well-being. Two lives with the same sum of momentary well-being may have different levels of lifetime well-being (and vice versa).

The difference between these views can be summarised thus. According to *additivists* about lifetime well-being (hereafter just 'additivists') a person's lifetime well-being *just is* the sum of their momentary well-being. According to *holists* about lifetime well-being (hereafter just 'holists'), factors over and above a person's total momentary well-being *may* play a role in determining their lifetime well-being. Applied to the case of Uppi and Downey the additivist will say that Uppi and Downey's lifetime well-being must be the same. By contrast the holist will say that it does not necessarily follow from their having equal momentary well-being that their lifetime well-being is equal.

There are many ways to be a holist about lifetime well-being. By far the most common holist view is:

Shape of a life hypothesis: Other things being equal, the lifetime well-being of an uphill life is greater than the lifetime well-being of a downhill life.

Those who subscribe to the shape of a life hypothesis (hereafter just 'shape of a life') think that an equal quantity of momentary well-being results in greater lifetime well-being if the momentary well-being *increases* over the course of the life.

If the shape of a life hypothesis is true then holism is true. But the *converse* is not true. That is, holism could be true even if the shape of a life hypothesis is false. To see why, here are two alternative hypotheses which, though distinct from shape of a life, would entail that holism is true:

End of a life hypothesis: Other things equal, the lifetime well-being of a life that is above a certain momentary well-being threshold at its end is greater than a life that ends below that threshold.

Never hitting rock-bottom hypothesis: Other things equal, the lifetime well-being of a life that never falls below a certain momentary well-being threshold is greater than the lifetime well-being of a life that ever falls below that threshold.

There are two other ways for holism to be true. And there are limitless other ways in which one could think that lifetime well-being is determined by more than the sum total of momentary well-being (each of which would be sufficient to make one a holist on this question). Though each of 'End of a life' and 'Never hitting rock-bottom' seems interesting and worth further exploration, in this chapter we will focus exclusively on holists who adopt the shape of a life hypothesis. Our guiding question is whether this hypothesis is plausible and significant.

Uppi and Downey's lives precisified

Let us return now to the case of Uppi and Downey. Let us use this graph to represent their levels of momentary well-being:

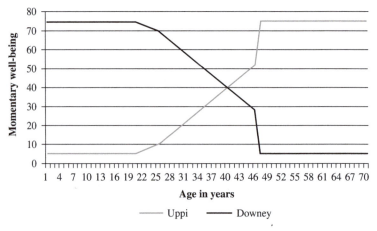

Figure 7.1 Uppi and Downey's momentary well-being across their lives.

(If you find this implausible, feel free to make whatever modifications you think necessary to the description of Uppi and Downey's lives for these representations to be accurate.)

What do we see from this? Well, we see that Uppi and Downey's lives are perfect mirror images with respect to their *momentary* well-being. Uppi's life starts off exactly as badly as Downey's ends (and vice versa) and Uppi's life improves at the same rate at which Downey's declines. Uppi and Downey's lives therefore have exactly equal total levels of momentary well-being.

If additivism is true, the fact that Uppi and Downey have equal total momentary well-being means that they must have equal *lifetime* well-being also. By contrast, if holism is true, then it does not *necessarily* follow from Uppi and Downey having identical totals of momentary well-being that they have identical levels of lifetime well-being (Uppi's lifetime well-being could be higher, for example).

Now, here is a question: if Uppi and Downey's levels of momentary well-being are as represented in the graph above, do you think their *lifetime* well-being was necessarily identical, that their lives were equal in prudential value?

Those who hold the shape of a life hypothesis will say that, in virtue of its going uphill, Uppi's lifetime well-being is higher than Downey's and that this is because of the uphill shape of Uppi's life. For the rest of this chapter we will assess the plausibility of the shape of a life thesis.

7.3 Assessing the shape of a life hypothesis: two additivist objections

In order to assess the shape of a life hypothesis we should examine objections to it. These are objections given by the additivist, as reasons to stick to additivism rather than adopting the shape of a life hypothesis.

Objection 1: Wrong kind of evaluation

A first way that the additivist might object to the shape of a life claim is by arguing that our tendency to endorse the shape of a life hypothesis when thinking about cases like Uppi and Downey stems from a failure to keep in clear view the relevant *kind* of evaluation. The problem, the additivist may urge, is that we conflate issues such as how good a *story* some life makes, with judgements of lifetime well-being. The additivist wielding this objection might urge that Uppi's is a better *story* – it is more uplifting, for example – but that this is not the same thing as its being a better life for Uppi to live.

Is this a good objection? Certainly it does seem plausible that in many ways an uphill life yields a better story of a life. And one might worry that we are conflating the quality of the *story* of a life with the quality of the *life* within the story. It also seems possible that we are mistaking a judgement of lifetime well-being with a judgement of how successful a life is. It is easy to think that an uphill life is more *successful*, because successes in adult life are more important than those in childhood. To use the case of Uppi and Downey, you might think that the successes that Downey enjoys in childhood are less important than Uppi's successes in adulthood. If we are guilty of mistakenly thinking about which is the more successful life, *that* might be why we think Uppi's life goes better.

However, with these kinds of objections we very quickly reach an impasse. Even if we might sometimes conflate the (aesthetic) value of a life (for example the quality of the story it would yield) or its successfulness with its prudential value, I take it that the intuition that the uphill life goes better is not simply a matter of making the wrong kind of evaluation. For whilst this objection does show that we need to be careful to focus on the right kind of evaluation (prudential, and not aesthetic) it seems implausibly uncharitable to think that *all* of the attraction that the shape of a life hypothesis has stems from the failure to distinguish these (or other distinct kinds of evaluations).

Objection 2: Debunking the shape of a life hypothesis

A common additivist objection is that the shape of a life hypothesis is not the right lesson to draw from cases such as Uppi and Downey. This is because, so the objection goes, all of the extra lifetime well-being in an uphill life can be traced to differences in *momentary* well-being. That is, the reason why uphill lives are better is that uphill lives have greater *momentary* well-being in virtue of being uphill. So whilst uphill lives do go better, this is not because of their shape per se but rather because of the extra *momentary* well-being that their being uphill brings about. Here is an analogy to motivate this idea. Take the following case:

> **Interesting in-laws**: You are meeting your in-laws for the first time and they insist on taking you to an experimental restaurant with a 10-course tasting menu run by a philosopher. The restaurant's distinct selling point is that, upon your arrival, the waiter flips a coin and you get either the 'uphill' experience or the 'downhill' experience. On the uphill experience you begin the meal with something quite unpleasant before the dishes gradually improve all the way to fine dining. On the downhill experience you eat the exact same dishes but in the reverse order.

Suppose the waiter has now flipped the coin and it comes up…'uphill'. How do you feel? Relieved, right? But why so? You are going to eat the exact same dishes either way. Doesn't that mean that your evening is just as good either way?

The answer seems to be no. It is highly plausible that it is more unpleasant/ painful to eat progressively *worse* food than to eat progressively *better* food. For one thing, suppose you are on course five. You will, on the uphill menu, know that what you are currently eating is better than anything that came before and that every subsequent dish will taste better than this. You will feel good (glad or relieved or happy for example) about this fact.

By contrast, on the downhill menu, you know that this is the *worst* dish you have had so far and that things only get *worse* from here. You will feel *bad* about this fact. Plausibly, then, you feel better at course five on the uphill menu than on the downhill menu. And the same for many, if not all, of the intermediate courses.

What does this show? Why might someone think that this kind of pheno-menon casts doubt on the shape of a life hypothesis? Its significance is that it shows that an uphill sequence of events is more enjoyable and that taking some uphill sequence and rearranging it into a downhill one does *not* preserve the total enjoyability of the sequence. An additivist might claim that an analo-gous phenomenon is true of lives that are uphill and downhill. For example, when your momentary well-being increases, you feel good about that fact ('I'm so much better off than I used to be!'). One very often feels good about improvements in momentary well-being. And such feelings are plausibly good for you. By contrast when your momentary well-being decreases, it is common to feel bad about that fact ('I'm so much worse off than I used to be!'). One can easily lament and be saddened by declines in momentary well-being. And such feelings are themselves plausibly bad for you.

From these kinds of observations, an additivist might argue that the uphill shape of Uppi's life is not why Uppi's life goes better than Downey's. Rather, Uppi's life goes better than Downey's because Uppi's *momentary* well-being will be higher, because uphill lives tend to have greater *momentary* well-being as a result of an agent's reactions to their going uphill. To put the claim more succinctly:

> **Debunking explanation**: Uppi and Downey's levels of momentary well-being do *not* sum to the same amount. Uppi's total momentary well-being is greater, because an improving life has extra goods in virtue of being uphill, and *that* is why her lifetime well-being is higher.

Is this a good objection? This objection is in some ways unresponsive to the case of Uppi and Downey. This is because it relies on rejecting the momentary well-being levels that were *stipulated* to be true of the case, based on the case descriptions (Figure 7.1). Nevertheless, this objection highlights two important points.

First, that it is very important when thinking about these issues that we really do make sure to hold fixed the *total* momentary well-being of each life. We have to be sure to compare lives that have the same total momentary well-being.

Second, the kinds of phenomena mentioned above mean there are lots of reasons for thinking that this will be *hard* and lots of reasons why there will be a difference in total momentary well-being when we give descriptions of uphill and downhill lives. We need to ensure that we do not overlook these good and bad feelings that can occur within uphill and downhill lives.[4]

The issues here are subtle so let me recap one last time. When given the descriptions of uphill and downhill lives like Uppi and Downey's lives, a common reaction is that the uphill life goes better. A major question is *why* that is true (assuming that it is). Is it because additivism is true and the uphill life, one like Uppi's, contains more *momentary* well-being? Or is it because the shape of a life hypothesis is true, so even if their total sums of momentary well-being are equal, an 'uphill', improving life like Uppi's is better simply in virtue of taking that shape?

How will a holist reply? Well, they should acknowledge that we need to be careful in specifying the cases to make sure we really are comparing lives with equal total momentary well-being. But they will likely say that when we make sure to do this, it is *still* the case that uphill lives are better.

7.4 Assessing the shape of a life hypothesis: one final additivist objection

Objection 3: Uphill shape is worth little or nothing

Here, I think, is a powerful objection that the additivist can wield against the shape of a life hypothesis: *if* the shape of a life really provides a separate, independent, contribution to lifetime well-being, over and above momentary well-being, then there should be *some* degree of momentary well-being that it would be lifetime-well-being-enhancing to forgo, in order to have an uphill life. But this is implausible, as shown by the following case:

> **Charlotte's child**: Charlotte is having a child (a boy). She is making plans for the future and determines that she has a choice about how to provide for this child in childhood. She can either:
> (option 1) give the child a very good childhood but at the expense of starting a pension fund for the child. The effect of this would be higher momentary well-being in childhood and lower momentary well-being in the child's dotage.
> (option 2) use her money to give the child a less good childhood but a much better dotage, by starting a pension fund for him.

Imagine that the child's momentary well-being levels in these two scenarios are as follows:

Table 7.1

	Option 1	Option 2
0–18	50	40
18–36	50	50
36–54	50	50
54–72	50	80
Total	200	220

When we compare options 1 and 2 it is clear that option 2 is the one where Charlotte's child has greater momentary (and lifetime) well-being. He has a little less momentary well-being in childhood but gains more than he loses in her retirement years. Doing so thereby gives him a higher total momentary well-being and greater lifetime well-being.

However, suppose that before Charlotte had the chance to decide on either option 1 and option 2, option 2 ceases to be available (suppose, for example, that all the pension schemes close). If the shape of a life hypothesis is true, all is not lost. This is because there would still be *another* way for Charlotte to enhance her child's lifetime well-being – she could make it the case that her child's life has an uphill trajectory. How might she do that? Charlotte could bring it about that he has a slightly worse childhood. (Not by doing anything cruel or horrible. Rather, instead of spending money on lovely holidays, which would be extremely fun, she could just burn the money instead, or simply choose to live in a less fun part of the city.) What would this mean? Well, if we hold fixed the momentary well-being of the child's later years, his momentary well-being in childhood being lower would give his life an uphill trajectory. And if the shape of a life hypothesis is true, Charlotte's child's lifetime well-being would be enhanced by his life having this uphill character. To see the point, imagine that the child's momentary well-being levels in these two scenarios are as follows:

Table 7.2

	Option 1	*Option 3*
0–18	50	40
18–36	50	50
36–54	50	50
54–72	50	50
Total	200	190

With option 1 there is no uphill shape to Charlotte's child's life at all (nor a downhill shape). Thus his lifetime well-being receives none of the benefits of having an uphill shape. By contrast, in option 3, there *is* an uphill shape. What is unusual is that the uphill shape is brought about by having a worse early period rather than a better, later, period.

How does this bear on the shape of a life hypothesis? The key question is whether Charlotte's child's lifetime well-being is greater in option 1 or option 3.[5] If the shape of a life hypothesis is true and so having an uphill shape contributes to lifetime well-being, then we should expect option 3 to have greater lifetime well-being than option 1.[6] The problem is that it does not seem plausible that Charlotte's child's lifetime well-being is higher in option 3. In fact, it seems very plausible that his life goes *worse* in option 3, that his lifetime well-being is *lower*.

How might a defender of the shape of a life hypothesis respond? One problematic response would be to claim that deliberately giving your child a worse childhood is *cruel*. The problem with this objection is that it assumes that the sacrifice that generates the uphill trajectory is not beneficial to the child (in terms of lifetime well-being). But if the shape of a life hypothesis is true then Charlotte's actions, in giving her child's life an uphill trajectory, precisely are beneficial. They enhance his lifetime well-being.

A slightly better response that the defender of the shape of a life hypothesis can make is to point out an implicit assumption in the above argument – that the shape of a life hypothesis is true only if having an uphill shape to one's life is worth more to lifetime well-being than *10* units of momentary well-being. They might then argue that they are not committed to that claim but only to the claim that an uphill shape contributes to well-being to *some* degree (perhaps a lesser degree than 10 units of momentary well-being).

This reply correctly identifies a background assumption of the example – namely that the shape of a life hypothesis is true only if having an uphill shape to one's life is worth more to lifetime well-being than *10* units of momentary well-being. The trouble with this reply is that it plays into the hands of the opponent, by conceding that the shape of a life is not worth very much. If the uphill shape is not even worth the 10 units of momentary well-being that Charlotte's child misses out on, is it a significant good at all? And should we not then be sceptical that an uphill shape actually does independently contribute to lifetime well-being?

If it is true, given the stipulations above, that Charlotte's child's lifetime well-being is higher in option 1 we seem to have discovered that an uphill shape contributes to lifetime well-being very little, if it contributes anything at all. An additivist can then use this as evidence that we were mistaken to think of uphill shape as making a contribution to well-being. They might claim that, given the tendency for uphill lives to have greater momentary well-being (for the reasons identified in objection 1) we should be especially sceptical that the shape of a life matters independently. From thinking about the case of Charlotte's child, we know that the shape of a life does not make a significant contribution to lifetime well-being and we also know that there are lots of ways in which uphill and downhill lives could fail to have equal momentary well-being. Thus, the additivist will claim, we should reject the shape of a life hypothesis.

These issues are subtle, so let me give a summary of the main dialectical moves. We want to know whether a life has higher lifetime well-being simply in virtue of having an uphill shape. Our initial focus was on two lives with different shapes but with *equal* total momentary well-being. That seemed justi-fied to make sure that we were detecting a difference that was not traceable to a difference in momentary well-being. However, by looking instead at lives with *unequal* total momentary well-being we can ask the important question of *how* beneficial an uphill shape is (when measured in terms of momentary well-being). But when we do this it seems that an uphill shape is worth very little, in terms of momentary well-being (as evidenced by option 3 not plausibly being better for Charlotte's child than option 1). It seems that it is not lifetime well-being enhancing to sacrifice even comparatively small amounts of momentary well-being to give a child's life an uphill shape. And that is reason to think that an uphill shape is not in fact a separate contributor to lifetime well-being and that we should reject the shape of a life hypothesis.

7.5 Conclusion

In this chapter we have examined the shape of a life hypothesis. We looked at three objections that it would be natural for an additivist to give as reasons to reject the hypothesis and accept additivism instead. If the third objection was even broadly correct, it seems that an uphill shape does not make a significant difference to one's lifetime well-being. And perhaps the additivist is right to claim that our tendency to think of uphill lives as better reflects either a failure to keep in mind the relevant kind of evaluation or a failure to ensure that we are holding fixed the total amount of momentary well-being.

However, there is still much to think about here. For as we saw earlier, there are many ways to be a holist. And at least one of the other holistic claims – the end of a life hypothesis – would, if true, generate the result that Uppi's life went better than Downey's. So the additivist has at least one more competitor to fight, to show that lifetime well-being is not independently affected by how one's life is at its end.

Comprehension questions

1   Why is objection 1 pretty unresponsive to the case of Uppi and Downey?
2   Which of these claims is true, if any?:

   a   If holism is true then the shape of a life hypothesis is true.
   b   If the shape of a life hypothesis is true then holism is true.
   c   If the shape of a life hypothesis is false then additivism is true.
   d   If additivism is true then the shape of a life hypothesis is false.

3   Could the never hitting rock-bottom hypothesis generate the result that Uppi's lifetime well-being is higher than Downey's? If so, how? If not, why not?

Further question

1   Suppose that the shape of a life hypothesis defender replies to objection 3 by pointing out that Charlotte's child's life will only be slightly uphill (that is, that it does not have a very steep climb). Would this be a good way to reply to the objection? How might the additivist reply?

Notes

1   Why go into so much detail? The reason is because it is easier to think about these issues, I think, if we actually spell out why the lives go up and downhill. But one might worry that going into the details introduces distractions.
2   Notice that we have not yet given any particular value to their well-being at any point in their lives.
3   You might instinctively be inclined to a view about the relation between these two things – that momentary well-being fully determines lifetime well-being.
4   For discussion of this kind of issues, see Feldman (2004: chapter 6).
5   Ignore any other possible actions she could perform. The relevant question is what to say about option 3 as compared with option 1.
6   Actually, that is not *quite* right, for reasons I explain very shortly. Namely that one might think that an uphill shape has some value but less than 10 units of momentary well-being.

References

Dorsey, Dale (2015). 'The Significance of a Life's Shape'. *Ethics*, 125(2): 303–330.
Feldman, Fred (2004). *Pleasure and the Good Life: Concerning the Nature, Varieties and Plausibility of Hedonism* (Clarendon Press).

Glasgow, Joshua (2013). 'The Shape of a Life and the Value of Loss and Gain'. *Philosophical Studies*, 162(3): 667–669.

Hooker, Brad (2015). 'The Elements of Well-Being'. *Journal of Practical Ethics*, 3(1): 15–35.

Raibley, Jason (2012). 'Welfare Over Time and the Case for Holism'. *Philosophical Papers*, 41: 2.

Raibley, Jason (2016). 'Atomism and Holism in the Theory of Personal Well-Being' in G. Fletcher (ed.), *Routledge Handbook of Philosophy of Well-Being* (Routledge).

Rosati, Connie (2013). 'The Story of a Life'. *Social Philosophy and Policy*, 30(1–2): 21–50.

Slote, Michael (1982). 'Goods and Lives'. *Pacific Philosophical Quarterly*, 63: 311–326.

Velleman, David (1991). 'Well-being and Time'. *Pacific Philosophical Quarterly*, 72(1): 48–77.

8 Well-being and death

8.1 Introduction

So far we have focused mostly on theories of what is good for us and then, in the previous chapter, we looked at the question of whether how well our lives go as a whole is determined simply by how well they go at each point. But I would be very surprised if you have not asked yourself the following question: Is *death* bad for me? After all, we are just as interested (perhaps more interested) in this question as in the question of whether pain is bad for us, or whether it is bad for us to have our desires frustrated. In this last chapter, I will turn to examining whether death is bad for us. I will spend the rest of this section on some preliminary issues. We will then (§2) look at reasons to think that death is a harm, or that it is not a harm. In §3 we will look more closely at what is meant by 'death' in the context of the question of death and harm and I will also introduce an analysis of harm. In the next sections (§4–5) we use these understandings of what can be meant by 'death', and of what harm is, to assess the objections to the claim that death is a harm. The tentative conclusion is that there are good objections to one interpretation of the harm thesis but that there is another interpretation of the harm thesis, one under which there is a plausible case that death is sometimes a harm.[1]

Take this claim: death is bad for us. Before trying to determine whether this claim is true we need to resolve an ambiguity. For here are two different things that might be meant by the claim that death is bad for us:

a Death is always a harm. (Death is non-instrumentally bad for *everyone* who dies.)
b Death is sometimes a harm. (Death is non-instrumentally bad for at least some people who die.).

(Henceforth I often omit the 'non-instrumentally', for the sake of readability. All claims about what is bad for should be taken to be about what is non-instrumentally bad for, unless otherwise specified.)

Notice that (a) is a logically stronger claim. If (a) is true then (b) is true but not vice versa. For the purposes of this chapter I will focus explicitly only on the weaker claim (b). From now, I am interested in whether death *can* be bad for someone, whether it is *ever* bad for anyone. For brevity, I will refer to this as the 'harm thesis':

Harm thesis: death can be bad for people.

As I explain below, I suspect that the most plausible view of whether death can be bad for someone will show that it is not in fact bad for everyone.

8.2 Why think death can be bad for us? Why think that it can't?

If you are asked *why* death can be a harm, you might be puzzled, at least at first. We find it very natural to think that death is bad for us. But here are some justifications that we might appeal to, in support of the harm thesis.

How death makes us feel

We have negative responses to things that are bad for us.[2] We fear and dread things that are bad for us, such as pain. We do the same with death. We *fear* death, we *dread* death. We are *saddened* by our friends being in pain and we are saddened by our friends dying. How we feel about death is evidence that death is bad for us. If death is not ever bad for us then, arguably, we should, and would, feel differently about it.

How we behave with respect to death

We make great efforts to avoid things that are bad for us, such as pain. We also make great efforts to avoid death. And just as we make great efforts to avoid things that are bad for our friends, we make great efforts to avoid the death of our friends. Our taking steps to avoid death is evidence that death is bad for us. If death is not ever bad for us then, arguably, we should, and would, make less effort to avoid death.

Death deprives us of good things

The dead have none of the things that are good for us. There is no pleasure (or friendship or happiness or...) for the dead. Thus death is bad for us because we will lack these good things.

These are some of the reasons we might appeal to in order to support the harm thesis. Why then might someone deny that death is a harm?

Objections to the harm thesis

Here are three arguments someone might give against the harm thesis and in support of the view that death is not bad for us.

(Objection A) One is not there to be harmed by death

One reason to doubt that we are harmed by death stems from the claim that when we are dead we do not exist to suffer any harm and that makes harm impossible. Let us spell this out as an argument:

i One can only be harmed by something if one exists.
ii If one is dead then one does not exist.

Thus,

iii One cannot be harmed by death.[3]

(Objection B) Symmetry with the time before our lives

A second reason to doubt that we are harmed by death relies on the observation that before our lives began we did not exist, coupled with the claim that non-existence is just the same, evaluatively speaking, as our non-existence after our lives end. Let us spell this out as an argument:

a Non-existence before our lives began is not bad for us.
b Non-existence before life begins is relevantly like non-existence after life ends.

Thus,

c Non-existence after our lives end is not bad for us.[4]

(Objection C) Death helps us avoid bad things

A third reason to doubt that we are harmed by death is the mirror image of the third reason we encountered above. It observes that the dead have none of the things that are *bad* for us. There is no pain (or unhappiness or loneliness or...) for the dead. Thus death is good for us because we will lack these things.

Before turning to objections to (A)–(C) notice, first, that (C) is in tension with (A). If, as (C) suggests, death is good for us because it enables us to avoid bad things then we are capable of being harmed or benefitted even when dead, which is denied by (A). Thus one cannot consistently deploy both of (A) and (C) in support of the claim that death is not bad for us.

We should now examine possible replies to these objections (A)–(C) to the harm thesis. However, to understand the replies we need first to better understand what it is for something to *harm* someone and what is meant by 'death' in the harm thesis. Remember that the earlier statement of the harm thesis was:

> **Harm thesis**: death can be bad for people.

In the next section I look at these two issues – what it is for something to harm someone and what is meant by 'death' in the harm thesis. We will then (§4) apply these insights when examining possible replies to the objections to the harm thesis.

8.3 Death and harm

Death

Notice that 'death' is commonly used to refer to at least these two things:

a   The state of *being dead*.[5]
b   The *transition* from being alive to being dead [dying].[6]

These are clearly not the same thing. Once we have distinguished them we see that there are two distinct harm theses:

> **Harm Thesis A**: Being dead can be bad for someone.
>
> **Harm Thesis B**: The transition from being alive to being dead can be bad for someone.

Two important resulting questions are (1) *which* harm thesis is the most plausible? and (2) which of the theses do the objections above apply to? We examine this further in the next section.

Having now seen the possibility of two different harm theses, depending on what is meant by the term 'death', let us now look more closely at harm.

Harm

Earlier we came across the claim that death is bad for us because it *deprives* us of good things. I will pause briefly now to introduce an analysis of harm, one that involves the idea of deprivation.[7]

Here is a paradigm case of harming someone. You are driving to a party. I crash my car into you. The result: a broken arm and a trip to the emergency room for you. I have harmed you. Furthermore, there is a prudentially disvaluable state of you that is generated by my paradigmatically harmful action: your broken arm.

Here is a different case:

> **Dastardly David**: David is head of an academic department who needs teaching cover for the next academic year. His preference is to ask Beth, a talented postgraduate who is an excellent teacher (the alternative is a much worse choice). Before he gets the chance to ask Beth, David learns that (unbeknownst to Beth) she is about to be offered a prestigious long-term research fellowship by a local eccentric millionaire, one that would transform her career enormously. Knowing that to be eligible for the fellowship Beth must not have a job lined up for the next academic year, David meets with Beth and immediately offers her a one-year contract, requiring that she accept or decline on the spot. Beth accepts and, consequently, does not receive the research fellowship offer (and never learns that it nearly happened). Her future career goes ok but is much less stellar than if she had received the fellowship.

David harms Beth in this scenario. But unlike the car crash case – where there is a broken arm – there is no prudentially disvaluable state of Beth we can point to in explaining how David harmed her. This might make us worry that either (i) there are two different *kinds* of harm or (ii) that we must say that one of these was *not* in fact a harm. Option (ii) seems very unappealing. Beth is harmed by David's action and you are harmed by my crashing into you. How then can we account for the fact that there is a harm in both cases? What analysis of harm delivers that result?

The key is to think about the kinds of complaints that Beth could make about David's behaviour were it made known to her. Beth could say: 'I'd have been so much *better* off if you hadn't interfered! You prevented me from having a much *better* career and life!' The same is true in the car crash case. You could justifiably admonish me after the crash by saying that you *would* have been *better* off if I had not crashed into you, that your life would have gone better.

What this suggests is that harm is a matter of making someone *worse* off than they would otherwise have been. We can formulate such a theory of harm more precisely thus:

> **Harm**: Event E harms S if and only if E makes S worse off than they would otherwise have been (their level of well-being is lower than it would otherwise have been).[8]

This is a *comparative* account of harm. It says that harm is a matter of detrimentally affecting someone's life, that one harms someone by reducing their well-being compared with what it would otherwise have been.

This analysis gets the right results about both of the cases above. In the broken arm case you were harmed because in crashing into you I made you worse off than you would otherwise have been (because you have a broken arm and a trip to the hospital rather than attending the party as you would otherwise have done). And Beth is harmed because David's actions made Beth worse off than she would otherwise have been, given that she would otherwise have received the life-changing fellowship.

In the rest of the chapter I will assume that this comparative analysis of harm is broadly correct. We will now turn to replies to the objections to the harm theses.

8.4 Replies to objections (A)–(C)

Let us now examine the objections to the harm thesis:

(Objection A) One is not there to be harmed by death

The first objection to the harm thesis was that one is not present to be harmed by death. I formulated this as the following argument:

i   One can only be harmed by something if one exists.
ii   If one is dead then one does not exist.

Therefore,

iii   One cannot be harmed by death.

In the previous section we noted that there are two different things that can be meant by the word 'death':

a   The state of *being dead*.
b   The *transition* from being alive to being dead [dying].

Looking at Objection A, it seems possible that it equivocates on 'death'. By this I mean that the argument uses different senses of 'death' in the premises in a problematic way. Premise (ii) is plausibly a claim about the state of *being dead*. If so, the conclusion can only be a claim about *being dead*, if the argument is to be valid. We can make this clearer by slightly reformulating the argument as follows:

(i*)   One can only be harmed by something if one exists.
(ii*)   If one is dead then one does not exist.

Therefore,

(iii*) One cannot be harmed by the state of being dead.

When we disambiguated the word 'death' we noted that this meant that there are two harm theses:

Harm Thesis A: Being dead can be bad for someone.

Harm Thesis B: The transition from being alive to being dead can be bad for someone.

Having clarified Objection A in this fashion, it seems clear that the objection targets only Harm Thesis A. It provides reasons for thinking that the state of *being dead* cannot be bad for someone (on the grounds that when one is dead one does not exist). It thus provides an argument against Harm Thesis A. But the argument does not provide any grounds for rejecting Harm Thesis B. Harm Thesis B is a claim about dying, about the transition from being alive to being dead, and the putative harmfulness of this seems unaffected by the argument given that one exists for (at least part of) this transition.

Assuming that Objection A only targets Harm Thesis A, how good an objection is it? The argument seems valid and premise (ii*) is unimpeachable, given our starting assumption that people who are dead no longer exist. Thus if there is a problem with the argument it would have to be with the truth of premise (i*). One might urge, against premise (i*), that it begs the question against the person who accepts Harm Thesis A. The person who accepts Harm Thesis A might think that whilst something like premise (i*) is true for most harms (harms such as pains, etc.) death is a unique case. The harm in that case is precisely the harm of non-existence. What is harmful is *to be dead*.

Can we avoid a stand-off here? One issue we could explore is the extent to which the person who accepts Harm Thesis A can plausibly treat being dead as an exception to the plausible general principle that one can only be harmed by something if one exists. Another strategy that the person who defends Harm Thesis A could pursue is to point to *other* possible cases that violate premise (i). This may be such a case:

Poisoned Pierre: Pierre and Jill are planning to have a child. Due to difficulties conceiving in the past they had their sperm and eggs frozen. They decide that today is the day to go and unfreeze them and implant them into Jill, in order to conceive. With it being a long drive, they stop at a service station on the way to the clinic to get drinks. Unfortunately Walker, a jealous rival, seizes the opportunity to lace Pierre's drink with a slow-acting poison. Pierre subsequently dies when Jill is in the sixth month of pregnancy. Jill later delivers a little boy, Jon.

Walker's action results in the premature death of Pierre. Given how Pierre's life would have gone, Walker harms Pierre.

Walker also plausibly harms Jill. Suppose, also, that Pierre would have been a fantastic father to Jon. As a result of Pierre's absence, Jon's life goes less well than it would otherwise have done. Here is a question – did Walker's action harm *Jon*? On the face of it, it seemed to. Jon seems equally able to make the complaint to Walker that Jill can make: 'you made my life go worse than it otherwise would have!' Plausibly, then, Walker's action harmed Jon. But here is the interesting twist: on any plausible theory of when exactly Jon came into existence, he did not exist at the time when Pierre was poisoned. It thus seems that we have a counterexample to premise (i) – a case of someone who is harmed by an event that occurred when they do not exist.

Reply

How might a defender of Objection A reply? It seems unpromising to claim that actually Jon *does* exist at the time Pierre is poisoned. Perhaps they will claim instead that Jon was not harmed and provide some debunking explanation of our tendency to think of this as a case of harm. For example, perhaps the fact that Jon can make a similar complaint to the one Jill can make is not sufficient evidence to conclude that Jon was *harmed*.

Alternatively, and perhaps more promisingly, they might reply that Jon is not harmed by the poisoning – which *is* prior to his existence – but, rather, by the *effects* of the poisoning – Jon's growing up without Pierre – which occur when he does exist.

Here is how someone who is sceptical about premise (i) might reply. Suppose that Walker died very soon after he poisoned Pierre (in fact before Pierre had reached the fertilisation clinic). Now, if we are treating the harmful event as *growing up without Pierre*, we seem to have a situation where Walker harms Jon when *Walker* does not exist. After all, Walker does not exist when Jon grows up without Pierre.

It seems that the person who wishes to defend (i) has a countermove here. They can argue that this previous response mistakenly assumes that when the event that harms Jon takes place we could also say that *Walker harms Jon* at that time. But, so the person will reply, this is just a mistake. There is an agent, Walker, who sets in motion a sequence of events and, at the end of the sequence, we have a harmful event, Jon's growing up without Pierre. But this does not mean that we should say that (non-existent) *Walker harms Jon* when the event that harms Jon takes place. Rather there is an event – growing up without Pierre – and this occurs when *Jon* exists, satisfying premise (i), and Walker's absence at that point is of no significance.

There are many more things that could be said here, of course. I do not want to go further into these (very interesting) issues. Let us instead move on to assessing the second objection to the harm thesis, Objection B.

(Objection B) Symmetry with the time before our lives

Objection B was as follows:

a   Non-existence before our lives began is not bad for us.
b   Non-existence before life begins is relevantly like non-existence after life ends.

Therefore,

c   Non-existence after our lives end is not bad for us.

How might we reply to this?

It is plausible that there is also a risk of equivocation in this argument. Premise (b) is plausibly a claim about the state of *being dead*. It seems clear that the state of *being dead* is relevantly like the state of non-existence before one's life started. At both of these times one does not exist. However, the conclusion of the argument can be read in two ways. It can be read either as a claim about the state of *being dead* or as a claim about *dying*, the *transition* from being alive to being dead. The argument is valid only if the conclusion uses 'death' to refer to the same thing that 'death' refers to in the premises. We can tidy this up by reformulating the argument as follows:

a   Non-existence before our lives began is not bad for us.
b   Non-existence before life begins is relevantly like being dead.

Therefore,

c   Being dead is not bad for us.

When the argument is clarified in this way we see that it targets only Harm Thesis A. It provides a reason to doubt that thesis but does not target Harm Thesis B. The pre-life and post-life states of non-existence might be relevantly similar but there is a clear difference between *pre-life non-existence* and *dying*. One exists for (at least part of) this transition from being alive to being dead. It is thus highly unlike the state of non-existence prior to one's life beginning.

How successfully does Objection B target Harm Thesis A? The argument is valid so the problem, if there is one, must be in the premises of the argument. I expect that at least the majority of those who hold Harm Thesis A do not think that *pre*-life non-existence was bad for us, so they will accept premise (a).[9] Premise (b), by contrast, is controversial. The proponent of Harm Thesis A will likely retort that non-existence before life begins is *not* relevantly like being dead. One clear difference is that prior to life, one has never existed, whereas after one's life ends one does not exist but did so previously.

Here is an analogy that the proponent of Harm Thesis A might point to in support. Suppose you are at a wonderful party having a wonderful time but, looking for the bathroom, you take a wrong turn and get locked out. Your experience now, of not being at the party, is *not* relevantly like the state of not being at the party before you got there. It is true that, before, you were not at the party and now it is also true that, now, you are not at the party. But things are different. Now it is true that you are not at the party but that (a) you *were* at the party, and (b) you *would* be at the party still if you hadn't taken a wrong turn. Someone wishing to object to premise (b) might claim that the same kind of thing is true in the death case. The dead are people who *had been* alive and who *would be* alive if they had not died.

What might someone who wields Objection B say in response? One thing they might say is that the analogy points to a plausible difference in how one *feels* in the two circumstances but that this is illegitimate. After all, their claim is about being dead and one who is dead feels nothing. Thus, they might claim, this destroys the putative parallel. Non-existence before life, they might reiterate, is relevantly like non-existence after life. In both cases one feels nothing because one does not exist.

(Objection C) Death helps us avoid bad things

The third objection to the harm thesis was that death allows us to avoid things that are bad for us. In that way it is good for us (or, at least, not bad for us).

How can we respond to such an argument? Well, unlike the previous two objections this argument seems to target both Harm Thesis A and Harm Thesis B. Here is how one could use the idea against Harm Thesis A. Suppose that Josh is dead but that if Josh were alive he would be suffering a terrible fate. One might then say that it is good for Josh that he is dead now, given what would be occurring if he were alive. And the person who makes Objection C will claim that this is true of death in general. Those who are dead are benefitted by missing out on the bad things that would otherwise afflict them if they were alive. That is how one might use this avoidance objection against Harm Thesis A.

One can also use this kind of objection to Harm Thesis B. One could say, of someone who is dying, that they are benefitted by dying because of what they will avoid. Suppose that Ashley is dying and very close to death but that, if he were alive in two weeks time, a terrible fate would befall him. One might then say that it is good for Ashley to be dying, given what would occur if he were to carry on living. That is how one might use this avoidance objection against Harm Thesis B.

As noted above, Objection C, if used against Harm Thesis A, is in tension with Objections A and B. This is because, if Objection C is used against Harm Thesis A, it suggests that non-existent, dead people, can be benefitted and harmed by things (for example, that Josh, despite being dead, is benefitted by missing out on the fate he would have suffered if alive). But Objections A and B deny that this can be true of the non-existent (precisely on the grounds that they are non-existent). For that reason, I propose to leave aside Objection C as an objection to Harm Thesis A but evaluate the objection as an objection to Harm Thesis B (which I do in the next section).

8.5 Harm Thesis B

We saw earlier that there are *two* harm theses that can be reported by the claim that death is bad for us. We also saw that Objections A and B only target one of these: Harm Thesis A. I also suggested that Objection C could be construed as an objection to both Harm Thesis A and B. In this section I move to assessing Harm Thesis B:

> **Harm thesis B**: The transition from being alive to being dead can be bad for someone.

Notice, first, that Objection C – that death is good for us (or at least not bad for us) because it enables us to avoid bad things – is the mirror image of one of the arguments *for* the Harm Thesis, namely that death is a harm because it deprives us of the *goods* of life. Arguably, this suggests that whether death is a harm because of what it deprives us of, or enables us to avoid, will depend on the details of the particular person's circumstances. Whether death is a harm will depend on what someone's life was like and would have been like if they had not died. We can use the *comparative* analysis of harm introduced earlier to formulate a deprivation account of the badness of dying. According to that analysis whether some event harms someone depends on what their life would *otherwise* have been like. We can formulate this more precisely as follows:

> **Deprivation explanation of the goodness/badness of dying**: dying is bad for someone if the life that they would otherwise have lived was positive overall (i.e. if they missed out on a net positive amount of well-being). Dying is good for someone if the life that they would otherwise have lived was not positive overall (i.e. if they missed out on a net negative amount of well-being).[10]

This explanation looks plausible. It explains why we tend to lament someone's death in terms of what they *missed out on* and what they were denied. To test this theory further let us consider some of the results that it gives. Let us begin with these three cases:

> **Mance**: Mance is shot by a stray bullet, killing him instantly. If he had not been killed by the bullet he would have endured a prolonged period of torture followed by a much more painful death some years later.

> **Maisie**: Maisie is shot by a stray bullet, killing her instantly. If she had not been killed by the bullet she would have lived for 25 years, all at a very high level of well-being.

> **Michu**: Michu is shot by a stray bullet, killing him instantly. Michu was 90 at the time of his death and suffered numerous health problems giving him a

low, but slightly positive, level of well-being. If he had not been killed by the stray bullet he would have died in his sleep within a month.

Plausibly, Maisie's dying is *very* bad for her. She would otherwise have had a very long period of very good life. By contrast, Mance's dying is not bad for him. By dying when he does, he is spared a prolonged period of torture and a more painful death. Thus it seems plausible to think that dying was actually good for Mance. Finally, Michu's death seems bad for him but it seems much less bad than Maisie's is for her. Michu's death deprives him of some good life but of much less than Maisie is deprived of.

The deprivation account gives very plausible results in these cases. Does this show Objection C to be mistaken? Not exactly. It shows that Objection C correctly describes *some* cases – that some people (e.g. Mance) are benefitted by dying, because of the bad things that would have happened to them if their lives had continued. Where it goes wrong is in implicitly assuming that that is true of every case. That seems not to be true, given the possibility of cases like Mance, whose dying enables him to avoid a horrible fate and so seems good for him.

At the beginning of the chapter, I pointed out that one can hold harm theses of varying strengths. For example there are these two theses (modified to resolve ambiguity):

a   Dying is always a harm (Dying is bad for *everyone* who dies).
b   Dying can be a harm (Dying is bad for at least some people).

I have mostly focused on (b), because it is the weaker of the two claims. However, I suggested earlier that a plausible explanation of why (b) is true might also shed light on whether (a) is true. Plausibly, the deprivation account of why dying is bad does exactly this. Applied to the cases of Mance, Maisie and Michu it explains why dying is a harm for *some* people (Maisie, Michu) but not for everyone (Mance). And that seems like a plausible outcome. Our judgements about whether dying was bad for some person do seem sensitive to what that person missed out on or avoided.

8.6 Conclusion

In this chapter we examined the question of whether death can be a harm for anyone. We examined three sceptical arguments against the claim that death is a harm. These arguments differ as to which version of the harm thesis they apply to. Two of them provided serious objections to the claim that the state of *being dead* is bad for someone. The third showed that *dying* can be bad for someone. But it did not show that dying is always bad for everyone. According to a plausible analysis of harm – the comparative analysis – dying is bad for those who are deprived of future well-being. This seems to fit with, and plausibly explains, our judgements about cases of death. We judge that it is bad for some to die, because of what they miss out on, but that this is not true for all cases. Thus, we seem to have found that there are good grounds for thinking that whilst the state of being dead is not bad for anyone dying is in fact bad for some people. And it is bad for them because of what they are deprived of.

Comprehension questions

1   'Death is a harm.' Using the distinctions drawn in the chapter, how many different interpretations of this claim can you come up with? Which do you find most plausible?
2   Why does the comparative account of harm say that dying is bad for Maisie but not for Mance?
3   What possibilities do the Poisoned Pierre cases demonstrate?

Further questions

1   Suppose that my crashing into you prevented you from a more serious crash with a lorry where you would certainly have been killed. What does the comparative analysis of harm say about my action in such a case? Do you agree with the result?
2   Can you think of any alternatives to the comparativist analysis of harm? What merits or demerits do they have?
3   Suppose that dying is bad for us. Is there a time at which it is bad for us? What is that time?

Notes

1   As throughout, you should make up your own mind on these issues as we go along.
2   This is not immune to error – some people have phobias about non-harmful things.
3   Epicurus was perhaps giving this argument when he wrote: 'Death…is nothing to us, seeing that, when we are, death is not come, and, when death is come, we are not. It is nothing, then, either to the living or to the dead, for with the living it is not and the dead exist no longer.'
4   Lucretius was perhaps giving this argument when he wrote: 'Look back also and see how the ages of everlasting time past before we were born have been to us nothing. This therefore is a mirror which nature holds up to us, showing the time to come after we at length shall die. Is there any thing horrible in that? Is there anything gloomy? Is it not more peaceful than any sleep?'
5   There are multiple theories of when something is dead. For discussion see Luper (2009).
6   As noted by Luper (2009), one could also use 'death' to refer to the last part of dying.
7   I do not mean to suggest that this is the only philosophical account of harm nor that it faces no difficulties. But space precludes a full discussion of the others (see references). The comparative account of harm is widely held and intuitively plausible.
8   This kind of comparative, counterfactual account of harm faces questions such as how exactly to determine what someone's well-being would otherwise have been. These issues are too large and too complicated to deal with here.
9   I use this assumption in the interests of brevity.
10 For further discussion of this kind of account see Nagel (1970), Bradley (2009), Feldman (1991).

References

Death and harm

Blatti, Stephan (2012). 'Death's Distinctive Harm'. *American Philosophical Quarterly*, 49(4): 317–330.

Bradley, Ben (2009). *Well-Being and Death* (Oxford University Press).

Broome, John (2013). 'The Badness of Death and the Goodness of Life' in B. Bradley, F. Feldman and J. Johansson (eds.), *The Oxford Handbook of Philosophy of Death* (Oxford University Press).

Brueckner, Anthony L. and John Martin Fischer (1993). 'Death's Badness'. *Pacific Philosophical Quarterly*, 74(1): 37–45.

Feldman, Fred (1991). 'Some Puzzles about the Evil of Death'. *The Philosophical Review*, 100(2): 205–227.

Luper, Steven (2009). *The Philosophy of Death* (Cambridge University Press).

Nagel, Thomas (1970). 'Death'. *Noûs*, 4(1): 73–80.

Pitcher, George (1984). 'The Misfortunes of the Dead'. *American Philosophical Quarterly*, 21(2): 183–188.

Harm

Hanser, Matthew (2008). 'The Metaphysics of Harm'. *Philosophy and Phenomenological Research*, 77(2): 421–450.

Harman, Elizabeth (2009). 'Harming as Causing Harm' in M. A. Roberts and D. T. Wasserman (eds.), *Harming Future Persons* (Springer Verlag).

Klocksiem, J. (2012). 'A Defense of the Counterfactual Comparative Account of Harm'. *American Philosophical Quarterly*, 49(4): 285–300.

Rabenberg, Michael (2015). 'Harm'. *Journal of Ethics and Social Philosophy*, 8(3): 1–32.

Shiffrin, Seana (1999). 'Wrongful Life, Procreative Responsibility, and the Significance of Harm'. *Legal Theory*, 5(2): 117–148.

Shiffrin, Seana (2012). 'Harm and Its Moral Significance'. *Legal Theory*, 18(3): 357–398.

Thomson, Judith Jarvis (2011). 'More On the Metaphysics of Harm'. *Philosophy and Phenomenological Research*, 82(2): 436–458.

Conclusion

C.1 Summary of the book

In this book I have discussed hedonism, desire-fulfilment theory, objective list theory, the happiness theory of well-being, perfectionism and hybrid theories. I have also examined whether the *shape* of a life matters along with the question of whether death is bad for us.

Most of the theories of well-being that I have covered are theory *types* rather than specific theories. From this you can see that there is a vast range of different theories of well-being. Each of the specific theories (/types of theory) I examined had some virtues. There were, nonetheless, problems for each. Let me briefly remind you of *some* of the significant problems and challenges for the theories and theory types.

The main challenge to hedonism stems from the results it reaches in experience machine type cases. Hedonism is committed to the claim that *any* two lives with the same hedonic level also have the same level of well-being. But there seem to be cases where two agents have the same hedonic level and yet their levels of well-being differ.[1] A challenge for those attracted to hedonism is to provide a convincing argument against such 'experience machine' examples.

Whilst hedonism seemed to be weakened by treating an agent's experience, their hedonic level more specifically, as the only thing that determines their well-being, the desire-fulfilment theory had the converse problem. The simple version of the view allows *too many* things to be good for an agent. This is because it treats your desiring some outcome as necessary *and sufficient* for its being good for you. But there seem to be clear cases where agents desire things that plausibly are not, in and of themselves, good for the agent. A challenge for those attracted to desire-fulfilment theories is to provide a plausible restriction on the desires that are relevant. The restriction must also be well-motivated and enable the theory to avoid the charge that the relevant set of desires merely track what is desire-independently good for us.

Objective list theories face a number of significant tasks. Anyone attracted to the view needs to provide an account of *which* goods are on the list. To take the example of an objective list theory with friendship on the list, they need to explain why friendship is really non-instrumentally good for us, rather than instrumentally good for us on account of the pleasure it generates. They also face the challenge of providing a convincing explanatory account, an account of *why* those things are good for humans (or of explaining why such an account is impossible). They also need to show that their theory is not problematically *alienating*. In the chapter (and in the appendix) we saw some ways in which an objective list theory can argue that their account is not alienating. Making good on that claim is a significant job for anyone attracted to objective list theories.

A major challenge for those tempted to hold a perfectionist theory of well-being is to provide a plausible account of human nature to go into the theory. This needs to be independently plausible as an account of human nature and it must also, in conjunction with perfectionism, deliver plausible verdicts about what is good for humans. Finally, they need to show that human nature really does explain what is good and bad for us, that things are good for humans *because* they accord (/promote/etc.) our human nature.

Another kind of theory we examined was a happiness theory of well-being. In discussing this theory we saw no reason to think that happiness is not *a* prudential value. But we saw reasons to be doubtful that a happiness theory of well-being can remain a distinctive view of well-being and deliver plausible results. This is partly because, on a hedonic view of happiness, the theory risks collapse into hedonism. Alternatively, a life-satisfaction view seemed to face a problem of indeterminacy and delivering problematic results in some cases. A happiness theory of well-being is also vulnerable to experience-machine-type worries. There are thus a number of different challenges for those tempted by the view that only happiness and unhappiness contribute to, and detract from, well-being.

One other kind of theory we examined was hybrid theories of well-being. We did so in order to see whether 'going hybrid' will enable us to capture the merits and avoid the demerits inherent in non-hybrid theories of well-being. In fact, the two hybrid theories we examined ended up being vulnerable to the majority of the objections that each of the constituent theories were vulnerable to, without accruing advantages elsewhere. This was only limited evidence (because there were only two possible hybrid theories). But it does show that we should not hastily assume that hybrid theories of well-being have better prospects than non-hybrid theories.

The final two chapters of the book examined lifetime well-being and death. First we examined the shape of a life hypothesis – the claim that lives that increase in *momentary* well-being as they progress have greater *lifetime* well-being than those that decrease in momentary well-being, even when the total momentary well-being was equal. Whilst such a view certainly seemed plausible as a claim about some cases, we saw a major challenge to such views – that the value of an uphill life seems very slight, if genuine at all. This was brought out by considering cases where someone can choose to give a life an uphill shape. If having an uphill shape makes a significant contribution to lifetime well-being we should expect that it would be worth sacrificing a fair amount of momentary well-being to give a life an uphill shape. But that does not seem to be so. One lesson one might draw from this is that an uphill shape does contribute to lifetime well-being but not very much. The other, more sceptical, conclusion is that the shape of a life does not, itself, contribute to lifetime well-being (though it may tend to correlate with other things that do).

Finally, we looked at whether death is a harm. A necessary step in making progress on that question is realising that 'death is a harm' is ambiguous. There is a difference between the claim that death is *sometimes* a harm and the claim that it is *always* a harm. There is also a difference between claiming that the state of *being dead* is a harm and claiming that the process of *dying* is a harm. The main arguments against the claim that death is a harm seem to show, at most, that the state of being dead is a harm. The claim that *dying* can be a harm – and a harm because of the well-being that it deprives us of – seems plausible, seems to accord with a plausible view of harm, and also seems to plausibly explain and underpin our feelings about deaths (both our own and those of others).

C.2 Related topics

There are a great many topics connected to well-being that it was not possible to cover in this book but which are philosophically and practically important. Let me say a little about each of them, just to provide a brief synopsis and guide to future investigation.

It seems undeniable that what we morally ought to do is at least somewhat sensitive to the effects that our actions will have on the well-being of others. Many people go further than this, by endorsing welfarism – the view that well-being is the only thing that fundamentally matters, morally speaking.[2] One such view is *utilitarianism*, the view that an action is morally permissible if and only if it maximises total well-being.[3] But there are many other theories that take well-being to be important to morality, even if it is not the only thing that matters morally. These include consequentialism (the view that the goodness of outcomes is the only thing that matters morally) along with alternate views such as contractualism, deontology and virtue ethics.[4]

Many people agree that states should aim to bring about equality over and above mere formal equality (equality before the law). More generally, people tend to agree that states should aim to *promote* certain goods for citizens. If we agree that states should aim to promote certain goods, we still need to determine *which* goods they should aim to promote (and why it is those goods and not some other). Some think that states should aim to promote citizens' well-being. Others think that states should promote related, but distinct, goods such as happiness, resources (such as money), or capabilities, or needs. Why states should focus on well-being, or other goods, is an interesting question.[5]

Another issue is the extent to which the state, medical professionals, or private individuals may justifiably *interfere* in people's lives in an attempt to promote their well-being. Some think that such interventions are only problematic because of the possibility of the judgements being mistaken (that we may fail to correctly judge what would promote your well-being). Others, however, think that we should not interfere with your actions even if doing so *would* in fact enhance your well-being, that you should be left to your own devices even if that would lead you to have a lower level of well-being.[6]

The limits to intervention in the lives of others is also relevant to well-being through the harm principle. Those who accept the harm principle think that one may only restrict someone's liberty only in order to prevent harm to others. Others think that there are other grounds for restriction of liberty beyond harm, grounds that may include the prevention of offence or disrespect.[7]

Notes

1 See the case of Trudy and Flora in chapter 1.
2 For discussion see Dorsey (2016), Keller (2009).
3 For discussion see Fletcher (2013), Driver (2012), Smart and Williams (1973).
4 For discussion see Ashford and Mulgan (2012), Alexander and Moore (2015), Hursthouse (2013).
5 For discussion see Cohen (1989), Dworkin (1981), Sen (1980).
6 For discussion see Mill (1859), Conly (2013), Anderson (1991).
7 For discussion see Mill (1859), Feinberg (1984, 1985).

C.3 References

Alexander, Larry and Michael Moore (2015). 'Deontological Ethics'. *The Stanford Encyclopedia of Philosophy* (Spring Edition), Edward N. Zalta (ed.). http://plato.stanford. edu/archives/spr2015/entries/ethics-deontological, accessed 22 December 2015.

Anderson, Elizabeth (1991). 'J.S. Mill's Experiments in Living'. *Ethics*, 102(1): 4–26.

Ashford, Elizabeth and Tim Mulgan (2012). 'Contractualism'. *The Stanford Encyclopedia of Philosophy* (Fall Edition), Edward N. Zalta (ed.). http://plato.stanford.edu/archives/fa ll2012/entries/contractualism, accessed 22 December 2015.

Cohen, G. A. (1989). 'On the Currency of Egalitarian Justice'. *Ethics*, 99: 906–944.

Conly, Sarah (2013). *Against Autonomy: Justifying Coercive Paternalism* (Cambridge University Press).

Dorsey, Dale (2016). 'Welfarism' in G. Fletcher (ed.), *Routledge Handbook of Philosophy of Well-Being* (Routledge).

Driver, Julia (2012). *Consequentialism* (Routledge).

Dworkin, Ronald (1981). 'What Is Equality? Part 1: Equality of Welfare'. *Philosophy & Public Affairs*, 10(3): 185–246.

Feinberg, Joel (1984) *Harm to Others: The Moral Limits of the Criminal Law* (Oxford University Press).

Feinberg, Joel (1985). *Offense to Others: The Moral Limits of the Criminal Law* (Oxford University Press).

Fletcher, Guy (2013). 'Act Utilitarianism' in J. Crimmins (ed.), *Bloomsbury Encyclopaedia of Utilitarianism* (Bloomsbury Academic).

Hursthouse, Rosalind (2013). 'Virtue Ethics', *The Stanford Encyclopedia of Philosophy* (Fall Edition), Edward N. Zalta (ed.). http://plato.stanford.edu/archives/fall2013/entries/ethics-virtue, accessed 22 December 2015.

Keller, Simon (2009). 'Welfarism'. *Philosophy Compass*, 4(1): 82–95.

Mill, J. S. (1859). *On Liberty.*

Sen, Amartya (1980). 'Equality of What?' *Tanner Lectures on Human Values*, Vol. I. http://tannerlectures.utah.edu/_documents/a-to-z/s/sen80.pdf, accessed 22 December 2015.

Smart, J. J. C. and Bernard Williams (1973). *Utilitarianism: For and Against* (Cambridge University Press).

List of cases

I list here some of the cases that I use in the discussion and which readers may want to refer back to. They are listed in order of appearance in the text.

Raj on the Rollercoaster:
Raj is enjoying a rollercoaster ride. Suddenly, a bird flies into his face, which is very painful. After getting off the ride Raj is given some painkillers which numb the area and he feels no pain. His friend then buys him candy floss, which he loves, and pleasurably eats.

Trudy and Flora:
Trudy lives in New York. When not carrying on her ground-breaking research into stem cell treatment, she enjoys running marathons, working for a local charity, skiing, socialising with friends and spending time with her life partner and their children. She also somehow finds time to pen highly successful, critically acclaimed, novels. She enjoys great physical health and springs out of bed every morning full of joy and excitement. Now meet Flora. When Flora was born she was attached to a machine that produces sensory stimulation and that gives her very rich, vivid, and life-like experiences. She has the pleasurable experience of carrying on ground-breaking research into stem cell treatment, of running marathons, of working for a local charity, skiing, socialising with friends and spending time with her life partner and their children. She also has the experience of writing highly successful and critically acclaimed novels. She is kept physically healthy by the machine and she also has the experience of springing out of bed every morning full of joy and excitement.

The Stranger on a Plane:
On a plane from London to Madrid, Lucy meets Ben who tells her that he's going to a remote village in Spain to marry his childhood sweetheart, John. Lucy leaves

the plane desiring that Ben is successful in this and that he lives a happy life. This happens but Lucy never hears from them and never travels near there again (nor do they ever visit England).

Life on Mars:	In 2014, Hilary desires that there is life elsewhere in the universe. Unbeknownst to all humans (and only discovered after her death) there is life on Mars in 2014.
Stockholm Syndrome:	Phil is in a physically and psychologically abusive relationship. In time he stops desiring to leave his partner and his strongest desire is simply to always remain with his partner. His few remaining friends and his doctor, aware of his situation, give him opportunities to escape but he declines.
Miserable Maud:	Maud is a fully committed ascetic. She thinks that all pleasure is the devil's work and forbidden by her deity. As a result she desires to never feel pleasure and hates the idea of it. Unbeknownst to Maud, she has extremely pleasurable dreams on a nightly basis, dreams that she does not recall upon waking.
Negative Norman:	Norman is raised by a religious cult that convinces him that he is worthless and that he should not aspire to feel good about himself or his life. As a result he not only lacks self-respect and happiness but ceases even to desire these things.
Undecided Ursula:	Ursula lives a life full of enjoyable pursuits. She has many friends, she is successful in her career as a pilot and she has an active social life full of hobbies and fun. One day a psychologist, seeking to determine her level of happiness, asks her to rate 'how satisfied she is with her life as a whole' by choosing a point on a scale from very satisfied to very unsatisfied. Ursula replies: 'I don't understand the question. There are lots of ways of evaluating my life. Can you clarify?'
Undecided Ursula continues her day:	Having finished talking to the psychologist, Ursula continues her day. She has an exquisite, enjoyable, lunch. She drinks some wonderful beer which she gets great pleasure from. She plays ping pong with people at the bar. She then walks along the beach back home. When she gets home a migraine strikes. She has a horrible headache and feels pretty wretched. She decides to go and buy some painkillers. But on her way out the house she slips down the front stairs, breaking her finger. Fifteen minutes later she is discovered by a neighbour who gets her to hospital.

Satisfied Sunita: Sunita suffers from a range of severe mental and physical
                       disabilities. Her condition means that she rarely leaves
                       the house. She has no hobbies or interests nor does
                       she have any friends. She spends her time watching
                       gameshows.

Malicious   Melisandre 1 experiences pleasure when seeing people
Melisandres: and animals in pain. Melisandre 2 desires that people
                       and animals be in pain, desires that regularly get
                       fulfilled.

Sally's Self-Respect: Sally's upbringing left her with a low sense of self-worth
                       and self-respect. However, after a difficult youth, she is
                       successful in her career and in love. Her career success,
                       coupled with finding love, lead her to gradually develop
                       self-respect. However, at no point prior to acquiring this
                       self-respect did she desire it. She never gave it much
                       thought and, if she had considered the issue, she wouldn't
                       have recognised that she *lacked* self-respect and so
                       wouldn't have desired to acquire it.

Rae's Recital: Rae is a classical musician who will be performing at a
                       highly distinguished venue. Her perfectionist tendencies
                       mean that she practises continually for months with
                       meticulous care and attention. She desperately desires to
                       give a perfect performance. On the day it goes flawlessly;
                       her performance is magnificent. However, she does not
                       experience any pleasure in connection with the perfor-
                       mance. Her pre-performance nerves rob her of any
                       enjoyment in the build up. And during the performance
                       her focus is entirely on getting the music right. Then,
                       after the performance she remains so unconvinced that
                       it went well that she takes no pleasure from it.

Uppi's life and   Uppi and Downey are twins whose parents are tragically
Downey's life: killed within hours of their birth and who are then
                       separated and raised completely separately. Their lives
                       take very different courses. *Early years (0–20)* Uppi is
                       raised in poverty and has severe health problems that
                       are exacerbated by having to work full time cleaning
                       factories to support herself. She has no free time, few
                       material goods, little formal education, and no time for
                       friendships or play. She is miserable and exhausted
                       almost every day. Downey is raised by an affluent loving
                       family who live within a close-knit community. She
                       enjoys excellent education, she makes many firm friends,
                       she excels at sport and science regularly winning junior
                       olympiads and representing her country at football. She

is cheerful and happy almost every day. *Middle Years (20–47)* Uppi spends most of her 20s, 30s and 40s working in the factory. The work is still hard and the hours long but eventually stricter government regulations coupled with technological development means that the work gradually becomes less laborious. Her health gradually improves as a result of moving from manual work to operating a computer. Her wages increase as a result of equality legislation, enabling her to move to a less polluted area. She is finally able to enjoy life, bit by bit. She makes friends at the factory and in her local community. Each year goes a little better than the previous one. Downey goes to college at a prestigious American university. During her final semester she attends a party and meets George. Hitting it off with him immediately, they decide to drive to a nearby bar. On the way they are involved in a car accident in which a child is killed. She is found not guilty of causing death by dangerous driving but, as the driver, Downey is racked by guilt. She attempts to return to university and despite making some progress on her course, she is shunned by her peers in light of the accident. Her grades suffer, she is a depressed recluse but eventually she graduates with a mediocre degree. After college, she becomes a call-centre worker. She hates her job, lives at home with her parents, has no social life or interests and, though constantly haunted by the feeling that her early promise has been wasted, is unable to stick to any plan to get her life back on track. Each year is worse than the previous one. Eventually she has no self-confidence or sense that her life could be any better. *Last Section (47–70)* Aged 47, Uppi literally bumps into one of the suppliers to the factory. To apologise for knocking her over, the factory supplier offers to buy her dinner. She accepts. They get on very well and become good friends. Learning of her life and near-poverty, the supplier is moved to help Uppi. She gives her money to sort out her remaining health problems, and sufficient money to enable her to work part-time and to enrol in night classes in engineering. Uppi turns out to be naturally adept at engineering and is offered a full scholarship to a prestigious American university. There she excels at engineering, graduating *magna cum laude* and develops a number of rewarding hobbies and interests. She is also extremely popular, making many firm friendships and falling in love with a fellow mature student. After college, Uppi and her partner work for a charity that develops and distributes cheap, secure, housing to developing countries. They live in a welcoming secure neighbourhood and enjoy many hobbies and interests with their friends. Uppi's work is internationally recognised and she is invited to join many international organisations to advise on how to alleviate poverty and improve housing in developing countries. She is sufficiently affluent to have zero money worries. Upon hearing of her remarkable life-story she is persuaded by publishers to write an autobiography, which is well-received. She loves her job and is able to continue in advisory roles after her retirement (she is not the sort of person who could simply retire) before dying peacefully in her sleep at 70. Aged 47, Downey's well-meaning parents send her to a rehab clinic at an exotic location to try to break the cycle that she is in. There, finally, she reaches resolution over the accident and decides that, upon returning home, she will re-enrol in university and try to get her life on track. Unfortunately, when Downey is at the airport returning home from her exotic rehab clinic she is targeted by a drug trafficker who, unbeknownst to her, puts liquid cocaine in her luggage. This is detected and Downey is arrested. Deprived access to proper legal advice, Downey is forced to sign a confession under the false pretence of its being a contract to pay a small fine for her release. She is denied bail and is continually prevented from obtaining adequate legal representation. Eventually her trial is heard and she is found guilty of drug trafficking. Her sentence is 25 years. She spends the rest of her days in a squalid jail cell working in the prison kitchen for the pittance that she spends on prison-acquired addictions. She is miserable and exhausted almost every day and finally dies of an overdose at 70.

Interesting inlaws: You are meeting your in-laws for the first time and they insist on taking you to an experimental restaurant with a 10-course tasting menu run by a philosopher. The restaurant's distinct selling point is that, upon your arrival, the waiter flips a coin and you get either the 'uphill' experience or the 'downhill' experience. On the uphill experience you begin the meal with something quite unpleasant before the dishes gradually improve all the way to fine dining. On the downhill experience you eat the exact same dishes but in the reverse order.

Charlotte's child:	Charlotte is having a child (a boy). She is making plans for the future and determines that she has a choice about how to provide for this child in childhood. She can either: (option 1) give the child a very good childhood but at the expense of starting a pension fund for the child. The effect of this would be higher momentary well-being in childhood and lower momentary well-being in the child's dotage. (option 2) use her money to give the child a less good childhood but a much better dotage, by starting a pension fund for him.
Dastardly David:	David is head of an academic department who needs teaching cover for the next academic year. His preference is to ask Beth, a talented postgraduate who is an excellent teacher (the alternative is a much worse choice). Before he gets the chance to ask Beth, David learns that (unbeknownst to Beth) she is about to be offered a prestigious long-term research fellowship by a local eccentric millionaire, one that would transform her career enormously. Knowing that to be eligible for the fellowship one must not have a job lined up for the next academic year, David meets with Beth and immediately offers her a one-year contract, requiring that she accept or decline on the spot. Beth accepts and, consequently, does not receive the research fellowship offer (and never learns that it nearly happened). Her future career goes ok but is much less stellar than if she had received the fellowship.
Poisoned Pierre:	Pierre and Jill are planning to have a child. Due to difficulties conceiving in the past they had their sperm and eggs frozen. They decide that today is the day to go and unfreeze them and implant them into Jill, in order to conceive. With it being a long drive, they stop at a service station on the way to the clinic to get drinks. Unfortunately, Walker, a jealous rival, seizes the opportunity to lace Pierre's drink with a slow-acting poison. Pierre dies when Jill is in the sixth month of pregnancy. Jill later delivers a little boy, Jon.
Mance:	Mance is shot by a stray bullet, killing him instantly. If he had not been killed by the bullet he would have endured a prolonged period of torture followed by a much more painful death some years later.
Maisie:	Maisie is shot by a stray bullet, killing her instantly. If she had not been killed by the bullet she would have lived for 25 years all at a very high level of well-being.

Michu: Michu is shot by a stray bullet, killing him instantly.
                          Michu was 90 at the time of his death and suffered
                          numerous health problems giving him a low, but slightly
                          positive, level of well-being. If he had not been killed by
                          the stray bullet he would have died in his sleep within a
                          month.

Glossary

Here are brief descriptions of some of the theories, theses and objections discussed in the main text. This is intended only to be used in conjunction with the text.

Additivism about lifetime well-being   The thesis that a person's lifetime well-being is fully determined by their total amount of momentary well-being.

Alienation objection   The objection that a theory of well-being is unacceptable if it does not link well-being sufficiently closely to the agent's desires/concerns/affective states (or similar). What counts as a sufficiently close connection is a matter of debate. On one interpretation, only a theory of well-being which endorses 'Attitude Dependence' avoids being alienating.

Attitude-dependence   The thesis that a necessary condition of something being good for someone is that they desire it. For example, 'G is non-instrumentally good for S only if S desires G'.

Attitude-independence   The denial of the attitude-dependence thesis (see above). For example, 'it is not the case that G is non-instrumentally good for S only if S desires G'.

Base pleasures objection   The following type of objection to hedonism about well-being:

1   If hedonism is true then all pleasures contribute to well-being.
2   If all pleasures contribute to well-being then base pleasures contribute to well-being.
3   Base pleasures do not contribute to well-being.

Therefore,

4   Hedonism is false.

A slightly different form of base pleasure objection to hedonism is as follows:

1   If hedonism is true then all equal-sized pleasures contribute equally to well-being.

2   If all equal-sized pleasures contribute equally to well-being then base pleasures of a given size contribute to well-being as much as non-base pleasures of the same size.

3   Base pleasures of a given size do not contribute to well-being equally with non-base pleasures of the same size.

Therefore,

4   Hedonism is false.

Brute objectivism   A theory of well-being which both (i) rejects attitude-independence and (ii) holds that there is no substantive explanation of why X, Y, Z (whatever the theory claims these to be) are the only things that contribute to/detract from well-being.

Death   'Death' can refer to at least these two things: (a) the state of being dead. (b) the transition from being alive to being dead.

Debunking argument   An argument which attacks the epistemic credentials of a belief by reference to its origin. In colloquial form 'You only believe that because…'. For example:

1   Your belief that J stems from process P.
2   Beliefs from process P are illegitimate.

Therefore

3   Your belief that J is illegitimate.

Deprivation explanation of the goodness/badness of dying   The thesis that dying is bad for someone if the life that they would otherwise have lived was positive overall (i.e. if they missed out on a net positive amount of well-being). Dying is good for someone if the life that they would otherwise have lived was not positive overall (i.e. if they missed out on a net negative amount of well-being).

Desire-fulfilment   In the context of the desire-fulfilment theory of well-being, 'desire-fulfilment' does not refer to the state of feeling fulfilled. Rather, it refers only to the world being how the person desires it to be. So, if I desire e.g. that my house has safe wiring this desire is fulfilled if my house has safe wiring (irrespective of whether I believe it has safe wiring, or know that it has). Note that sometimes the theory is called the 'desire satisfaction theory' where 'satisfaction' is used in the same way that I am using 'fulfilment' (such that my desires can be satisfied without my feeling satisfied).

Desire-fulfilment theory   The theory which holds the following: (i) something is non-instrumentally good for you if and only if and because it fulfils a non-instrumental desire of yours (ii) something is non-instrumentally bad for you if and only if and because it frustrates a non-instrumental desire of yours.

End of a life hypothesis The thesis that, other things equal, the lifetime well-being of a life that is above a certain momentary well-being threshold at its end is greater than a life that ends below that threshold, even if the total momentary well-being is equal.

Experience machine A type of counterexample to hedonism made popular by Robert Nozick. Such cases point out that hedonism is indifferent to whether your pleasurable experiences are based on an illusion and then claims that this is an objection to hedonism.

Experience requirement The thesis that if something contributes to someone's well-being it must affect their experience in some way.

Explanatory objectivism A theory of well-being which both (i) rejects attitude-independence and (ii) holds that there is a substantive explanation of why X, Y, Z (whatever the theory claims these to be) are the only things that contribute to well-being.

Happiness 'Happiness' is sometimes used to refer to 'well-being'. Other times the word is used to refer to a condition of a person (which may or may not be hedonic or otherwise psychological). Here are some theses connected to happiness that appear in the main text:

> **Happiness theory of well-being** The theory of well-being which holds the following
>
> (i) All and only happiness is non-instrumentally good for us; (ii) All and only unhappiness is non-instrumentally bad for us; and (iii) A person's overall level of well-being (at some particular time, or over some period) is determined solely by their overall level of happiness.
>
> **Pleasure theory of happiness** A claim about the nature of happiness, namely that to be happy just is to have a hedonic level of H or above. To be unhappy just is to have a hedonic level of U or below
>
> **Life satisfaction theory of happiness** A claim about the nature of happiness, namely that one's degree of happiness just is one's degree of satisfaction (or reported degree of satisfaction) with one's life.

Harm Something harms someone if it makes them worse off. A major question: worse off than *what*? Different theories of harm supply different ways to draw the comparison. Other theories of harm reject the idea that harming is always comparative.

Harm thesis The thesis sometimes expressed by saying 'death is a harm'. To avoid ambiguity, I gloss this in the text as the thesis that death can be bad for people.

Hedonic level A person's overall balance of pleasure and pain

Hedonism about well-being The theory of well-being which holds the following: (1) All and only pleasure is non-instrumentally good for us. (2) All and only pain is non-instrumentally bad for us. (3) A person's overall level of well-being (at some particular time, or in some duration) is determined solely by the balance of pleasure and pain they experience.

Holism about lifetime well-being   The thesis that a person's lifetime well-being is not fully determined by their total amount of momentary well-being.

Hybrid theory of well-being   Any theory of well-being which specifies complex items as prudential values. For example, a theory which holds that enjoyed achievements alone hold prudential value.

Idealised desire-fulfilment theory of well-being   Some desire-fulfilment theories of well-being claim that well-being is determined by the fulfilment not of the desires of the agent as they actually are but, rather, of the desires that they would have in some improved circumstance. A general form of the view is as follows: something is non-instrumentally good for someone if and only if and because it fulfils the desires that they would have in ideal circumstances C (or that their idealised counterpart would have in C).

Knowledgism   The theory that holds that all and only knowledge contributes non-instrumentally to well-being.

Lifetime well-being   How well a person's life goes, with respect to well-being, as a whole. According to additivists a person's lifetime well-being is determined simply by their momentary well-being. According to holists this may not be the case.

Momentary well-being   A person's level of well-being/how well things are going for that person at a time or between two times.

Never hitting rock-bottom hypothesis   The thesis that, other things equal, the lifetime well-being of a life that never falls below a certain momentary well-being threshold is greater than the lifetime well-being of a life that ever falls below that threshold.

Objective list theory   Any theory which rejects attitude-dependence and so accepts attitude-independence (the view that it is not the case that G is non-instrumentally good for S only if S desires G).

Perfectionism about human well-being   The theory that holds the following: (i) the good life for a human is determined by human nature (ii) Human nature involves a specific set of capacities (iii) The exercise and development of these capacities is good for humans.

Pluralist theory of well-being   A theory of well-being which holds that there is more than one thing which non-instrumentally contributes or detracts from well-being. For example, the view that pleasure and achievement are non-instrumentally good for humans.

Prudential value/well-being/welfare   Something has prudential value when it contributes to a person's well-being or welfare, when it is good for them, when it makes their life go better than it otherwise would.

Qualitative hedonism   A form of hedonism which ascribes different levels of prudential value to equal-sized pleasures depending on their quality.

Scope problem   The objection to desire-fulfilment theories of well-being that we can have desires whose fulfilment is not plausibly good for us (such as desiring that the number of atoms in the universe is even).

Shape of a life hypothesis   The thesis that, other things being equal, the lifetime well-being of an uphill life is greater than the lifetime well-being of a downhill life.

Index

Taylor & Francis eBooks

Helping you to choose the right eBooks for your Library

Add Routledge titles to your library's digital collection today. Taylor and Francis ebooks contains over 50,000 titles in the Humanities, Social Sciences, Behavioural Sciences, Built Environment and Law.

Choose from a range of subject packages or create your own!

Benefits for you

- » Free MARC records
- » COUNTER-compliant usage statistics
- » Flexible purchase and pricing options
- » All titles DRM-free.

Benefits for your user

- » Off-site, anytime access via Athens or referring URL
- » Print or copy pages or chapters
- » Full content search
- » Bookmark, highlight and annotate text
- » Access to thousands of pages of quality research at the click of a button.

REQUEST YOUR **FREE** INSTITUTIONAL TRIAL TODAY	**Free Trials Available** We offer free trials to qualifying academic, corporate and government customers.

eCollections – Choose from over 30 subject eCollections, including:

Archaeology	Language Learning
Architecture	Law
Asian Studies	Literature
Business & Management	Media & Communication
Classical Studies	Middle East Studies
Construction	Music
Creative & Media Arts	Philosophy
Criminology & Criminal Justice	Planning
Economics	Politics
Education	Psychology & Mental Health
Energy	Religion
Engineering	Security
English Language & Linguistics	Social Work
Environment & Sustainability	Sociology
Geography	Sport
Health Studies	Theatre & Performance
History	Tourism, Hospitality & Events

For more information, pricing enquiries or to order a free trial, please contact your local sales team:
www.tandfebooks.com/page/sales

 Routledge
Taylor & Francis Group

The home of
Routledge books

www.tandfebooks.com